*Presented to:*

_____

*From:*

_____

*Date:*

_____

# GOD HAS SOUL

## CELEBRATING THE INDOMITABLE
SPIRIT OF AFRICAN AMERICANS

# HONOR **HB** BOOKS

*Inspiration and Motivation for the Seasons of Life*

An Imprint of Cook Communications Ministries • Colorado Springs, CO

08 07 06 05 04    10 9 8 7 6 5 4 3 2 1

*God Has Soul—Celebrating the Indomitable Spirit of
African Americans*
ISBN 1-56272-341-2

Copyright © 2004 Bordon Books

Published by Honor Books,
An Imprint of Cook Communications Ministries
4050 Lee Vance View
Colorado Springs, CO 80918

Developed by Bordon Books
Manuscript written by Niral R. Burnett
Cover designed by Koechel Peterson & Associates

# TABLE OF CONTENTS

# INTRODUCTION

God has placed a people in the Americas who exemplify an indomitable spirit. Arriving in chains and destined for centuries-long servitude, those once bound to forced subjection have risen to the most influential seats of world power. They have become business leaders, politicians, ministers, and missionaries—less than 150 years after they were freed from the physical chains that bound them. They are African Americans.

Among the multitudes of great African Americans, we find some of the most preeminent minds the world has ever known. Some were orators who, through the very sound of their voices, changed the world around them. Others produced innovations and inventions that influenced history. We also discover abolitionists who forced open the strongest links that bound their people in chains. There were still others whose accomplishments never made headlines, but who displayed the same unconquerable spirit that distinguished their African American brothers and sisters.

Webster's Dictionary defines "soul" as the immaterial essence, animating principle, or actuating cause of an individual life. There is no better way to describe the valiant but often uncelebrated African American heroes of our time and times past. Every American owes a debt of gratitude to these heroes, whose principles guided them in a cause that gave purpose and action to their individual lives.

*God Has Soul—Celebrating the Indomitable Spirit of African Americans* commemorates these heroes. It celebrates those African Americans who shone brightly in the midst of the darkest hours of their history. It celebrates the unyielding perseverance of those who refused to give up on life, even when surrender seemed to be the only option.

Through these inspiring stories you will be reminded that when God is on your side there is always a way to overcome, no matter how difficult life becomes.

## MAHALIA JACKSON—CHANGING THE FACE OF GOSPEL MUSIC

> *I loved best to sing in the congregation of our church—*
> *the Mount Moriah Baptist Church. All around me, I*
> *could hear the foot-tapping and hand-clapping. That*
> *gave me bounce. I like it much better than being up in*
> *the choir singing the anthem. I liked to sing the songs*
> *which testify to the glory of the Lord—those anthems are*
> *too dead and cold for me. As David said in the Bible*
> *"Make a joyful noise unto the Lord!"—that was me.*

—MAHALIA JACKSON

Of all the great gospel musicians of our time, there is perhaps no other single person who has influenced the sound of gospel music more than Mahalia Jackson. Born in New Orleans around 1911, she was the daughter of a Baptist preacher and a mother who worked as a maid. Sadly, her father was often absent from her life, and her mother died at a young age. Her extended family raised her.

Mahalia is said to have begun singing as soon as she could walk and talk. Her music career began in the world-famous jazz and blues music scene in New Orleans, Louisiana. She grew up during the Great Depression, when things were difficult for many—especially blacks in the South. In response to this depression, Mahalia sang. If it weren't for the hard times, we may never have heard her powerful voice fill the airwaves all over the country.

The trying financial times of the day led a group of young people from the Greater Salem Baptist Church to form a singing and entertainment group. They sang and performed skits for $1.50 per night. The money paid coal and mortgage payments. Soon their talent took them outside of the city, into surrounding states, and to national church conventions.

It seemed that the more opportunities this group of talented young people had, the more people began to resent them. They were accused of bringing jazz into the church. Many people did not appreciate the hand-clapping and the stomping. Some said that their performance was not dignified enough.

After the group performed in one church, the preacher stood up and condemned them for the style of music they sang. To this, Mahalia responded by saying that she had been born to sing gospel music. She reminded the pastor of the Psalm that says, "Oh, clap your hands, all ye people! Shout unto the Lord with a voice of triumph!" She exclaimed, "If it was undignified, it was what the Bible told me to do!" Mahalia kept on singing.

She became well known throughout the country for her unique presentation of gospel music. Her style was alive! When the freedom movements began among blacks with Martin Luther King Jr. as their foremost figure, Mahalia Jackson was among them.

The crowds were immense. People had gathered as far as the eye could see that warm day at the Lincoln Memorial. Mahalia sat waiting for her turn to address the crowd in song. Then, at the request of Doctor King, she began to sing the song "I Been Buked and I Been Scorned." As her voice began to fill the air, a great murmur came rolling back from the multitude. The song touched the hearts of countless thousands of people. Tears and laughter filled the air, and Mahalia began to shout for joy. The great multitude joined in worship toward God, singing, swaying, and clapping their hands. Ironically, this behavior was the very thing Mahalia had been criticized for years earlier, but the power of her voice and God's call upon her life were more than enough to quiet her critics.

After the minutes-long revival meeting, while Mahalia was still catching her breath from leading the congregation in song, Reverend Martin Luther King Jr. stood up and delivered the speech that made him famous. It could be that the power and conviction in the voice of Mahalia Jackson motivated him to raise his voice, and like never before, sound the alarm for freedom. From the moment she sat down, the Civil Rights Movement marched on in full force.[1]

## SAMUEL MORRIS—THE APOSTLE OF SIMPLE FAITH

Kaboo was the eldest son of the Kru tribe Chieftain. Being well-versed in the religion of his tribe, the Chieftain taught diligently the existence of a god of war, a god of sickness, a god of the lake, a god of cattle, and many others. He also taught the worship of the dead. Even as a young child, Kaboo made altars to appease these gods, filling them with food and other offerings. In his mind, his actions would protect him from the enemy tribe in the vicinity, the Grebos.

Despite his many sacrifices, the Grebos' attack eventually came. The Grebos killed many of the young men in the tribe, including Kaboo's best friend. This event shook Kaboo's faith in his gods, and he eventually conceded that they had no power.

Yet, this decision did not stop the Grebos from torturing him. In the midst of his torture, a bright light shone around him. The ropes dropped from around him, and a voice instructed him to run. And run he did, until nightfall. Not knowing where to go, young Prince Kaboo continued on his journey and became a fugitive in his homeland.

A few days later he stumbled into the yard of a small farm and was greeted by a man who had been kneeling on the floor of the porch. This young man was a Christian and immediately invited Kaboo to his church. During the church service, Kaboo received the love of Jesus into his heart. With that significant change in his life, his journey into greatness began.

Not long after his conversion, Kaboo became a man of prayer and soul winning. He taught and prayed often, and many unique things occurred as he spent time with God. He was a changed man, and he began to sense the call of God on his life. His hunger for God led him to travel across the Atlantic Ocean to a place called New York to see a man named Stephen Meritt. At only seventeen years of age, Kaboo changed his name to Samuel Morris, chartered a small vessel, and began his journey to the Americas.

During the six-month journey to New York, Samuel remained a man of prayer. Through his prayers, God healed a crippled cabin boy. In spite of his prayers and faith in God, Samuel endured repeated beatings while on the ship. In time, however, he witnessed the conversion of the abusive captain of the ship. The crewmembers began to realize that this young man had a gift of unusual spiritual power. They saw in Samuel a strength that was greater than the rough might of the crewmembers. Samuel continued to pray, and peace permeated the ship—a peace the crew had never experienced before. The ship arrived in New York still under the influence of this supernatural peace.

Disembarking only twenty years after the Civil War, Samuel found himself in a very segregated land. However, this young black man from Africa knew that he was called to preach the gospel wherever God sent him.

Upon arrival, Samuel hitchhiked to the headquarters of Stephen Merritt. Merritt was the director of a ministry called the Bethel Mission. When he found Stephen Merritt, Samuel approached with an unusual greeting: "I have come from Africa to talk to you about the Holy Spirit."

After hearing those words, Merritt invited Samuel to stay at his mission. Later that night, Merritt visited Samuel and was astonished to find that Samuel was not sleeping after his long journey. Merritt found Samuel in the chapel, crying out to God. With him in the chapel were seventeen men weeping and repenting of their sins. Seeing these men, Merritt knew that God had a great purpose in sending Samuel to him.

In time, Samuel became a sought-after minister of the gospel. Though uneducated by the standards of his new western culture, Samuel was used by God to bring many sinners to repentance. His fervent devotion to prayer and his mountain-moving faith set a powerful example and changed countless lives.

Because of his low tolerance for the harsh winter weather, Samuel Morris became extremely ill. In the final hours of his life, Samuel recognized that he had obeyed God's call and purpose for his life. Although he died at only twenty years of age, this former pagan teacher had been reborn in Christ and experienced the presence of the Holy Spirit as few ever do. He shared this presence with all who would receive.

The life of Samuel Morris clearly demonstrates that God often uses the most unlikely people to accomplish great things. His testimony poses a challenge to us all to honor God by being willing and obedient servants to His purposes, like young Prince Kaboo.

## Betsy Stockton—More Than a Servant

When she was only in her early twenties, Betsy Stockton found herself on her way to the Sandwich Islands along with twelve other missionaries en route to the southern tip of South America. The American Board of Commissioners of Foreign Missions had sent Betsy and her team, which consisted of herself and twelve men. Aside from being the only woman on the team, Betsy had another qualification that made her stand out as a significant member of this missionary trip. Betsy was a former slave. The law demanding the gradual emancipation of slaves in New Jersey did not go into effect until 1825. Yet God clearly answered Betsy's heart's desire when, soon after her conversion, her owner, Ashbel Green, set her free in 1816.

Betsy's master not only freed her from slavery, but also highly recommended that she become a missionary. He stated in his recommendation that she "was [better] qualified for higher employment in a mission, than domestick drudgery."[2] Her employer himself asked her to join him and his wife on a missionary journey. She would be a part of the journey as a teacher, not just a servant.

Betsy had a mastery of the Word of God as well as the English language. One person described her as "pious, intelligent, industrious, skillful in the management of domestic affairs, apt to teach, and endued with a large portion of the active, persevering, self-sacrificing spirit of a missionary." It was also noted by the same person that she had "a larger acquaintance with sacred history and the mosaic institutions than almost any ordinary person, old or young, I have ever known." Betsy's purpose was to reach her destination and serve her heavenly Master. Her willingness to overcome the odds and fulfill her life's purpose made her life noteworthy.

Although Betsy's ministry was short-lived due to illness, one significant achievement stands out from her time in the Hawaiian Islands. Soon after her arrival the king's son asked, through a translator, for her to teach him English. Betsy agreed. Not long after she began to teach him English, she began a school to teach other students English and Hawaiian.

As a missionary, Betsy played a major role in bringing the English language to Hawaii. If she had remained in the United States, she could have been a slave or a grossly underpaid servant. Her obedience to God's call took her across the globe, far away from the world she knew, to bring the love of Jesus to a group of people who did not know Him.[3]

We all have a similar responsibility to show God's love to a lost and hurting world. When we sense God calling us to trust Him more as we attempt something that appears impossible, the life of Betsy Stockton can serve as an inspiring example. She followed God into the unknown, stayed her course, and finished her race. It is certain today that her service and her undying faith secured her place in God's eternal kingdom.

## JARENA LEE—THE NEGRO WOMAN PREACHER

Every pulpit she sought remained closed to her. Whether the church consisted of blacks, whites, or any other race, she did not receive the opportunity to preach for one reason—she was a woman. In the early 1800s, it was highly unthinkable for an African American woman to have a preaching license. With the exception of various crusaders for the cause, women's rights remained out of reach to most. However, Jarena was not one to conform easily to the normalcy of such discrimination.

Jerena served as a maid from the age of seven and lived in a largely non-Christian home. She described her parents as "wholly ignorant of the knowledge of God." Her own conversion came through the conviction she felt after telling a lie while she worked as a slave. The Spirit of God convicted her so strongly that day that she promised never to tell another lie for the rest of her life. She made this promise just prior to her conversion.

"Go preach the gospel!"

These words rang in Jarena's spirit as she sought God one day. He continued to speak to her heart, telling her that He would put the words in her mouth and turn her enemies into her friends. Jarena told Reverend Richard Allen, the preacher for the African Society, of her experience and what God had told her. She expressed to him that she felt it was her duty to preach the gospel.

Reverend Allen respected her call but informed her that their discipline did not allow for female preachers. In her memoirs, Jarena spoke of her response to this news:

> *O how careful ought we to be, lest through our bylaws of church government and discipline, we bring into disrepute even the word of life. For as unseemly as it must appear nowadays for a woman to preach, it should be remembered that nothing is impossible with God. And why should it be thought impossible, heterodox, or improper for a woman to preach, seeing the Savior died for the woman as well as the man? If the man may preach, because the Savior died for him, why not the woman, seeing he died for her also? Is he not a whole Savior, instead of a half one, as those who hold it wrong for a woman to preach, would seem to make it appear?*

Eight years after Jarena submitted her application to preach, God again prompted her to preach the gospel. In her words, it was like "a fire shut up in my bones." Jarena again requested the help of Richard Allen, and he permitted her to hold prayer meetings in her own rented house. This was as much as he would do for Jarena, since ordination was not an option. In her meetings, she exhorted the people. The opportunity to exhort was all she needed in order to launch her ministry as a preacher of the gospel.

As Jarena sat in the Bethel Church listening to the minister in attendance, God inspired her to expound on a point he was making. At a moment when he, in Jerena's words, seemed to have "lost the

Spirit," she suddenly sprang up and began to give her exhortation. Richard Allen, also in attendance, stood up as well. At once, fear assailed her as she wondered whether he would expel her from the church. However, Jarena's words demonstrated to everyone in attendance her ability to labor in the gospel through preaching. That experience affirmed her calling, and her ministry began in earnest.

Starting in a house not far from where she lived, she began to travel and minister the gospel through prayer and exhortation. Many miraculous things happened at Jarena Lee's prayer meetings. Her words seemed to come straight from God himself. She began to receive invitations to minister the gospel in other places. Many people were set free by the message taught by the "colored woman preacher." Towards the end of her ministry, she penned these words:

> *I now conclude—by requesting the prayers of God's people everywhere, who worship in His holy fear, to pray for me, that I ever may endeavor to keep a conscience void of offense, either towards God or man—for I feel as anxious to blow the Trumpet in Zion, and sound the alarm in God's Holy Mount, as ever.*
>
> > *Though Nature's strength decay,*
> > *And earth and hell withstand;*
> > *To Canaan's land I'll urge my way,*
> > *At HIS Divine command.*
>
> *But here I feel constrained to give over; as from the smallness of this pamphlet I cannot go through with the whole of my journal, as it would probably make a*

*volume of two hundred pages; which, if the Lord be willing, may at some future day be published. But for the satisfaction of such as may follow after me, when I am no more, I have recorded how the Lord called me to His work, and how He has kept me from falling from grace, as I feared I should. In all things He has proved himself a God of truth to me; and in His service I am now as much determined to spend and be spent, as at the very first. My ardour for the progress of His cause abates not await, so far as I am able to judge, though I am now something more than fifty years of age.*

*As to the nature of uncommon impressions, which the reader cannot but have noticed, and possibly sneered at in the course of these pages, they may be accounted for in this way: It is known that the blind have the sense of hearing in a manner much more acute than those who can see: also their sense of feeling is exceedingly fine, and is found to detect any roughness on the smoothest surface, where those who can see find none.*

*So It may be with such as I am, who has never had more than three months schooling; and wishing to know much of the way and law of God, have therefore watched the more closely, the operations of the Spirit, and have in consequence been led thereby. But let it be remarked that I have never found that Spirit lead me contrary to the scriptures of truth, as I understand them. "For as many as are led by the Spirit of God are the sons of God" (Romans 8:14).*[4]

Jarena Lee was an incredibly bold woman. Even through hostilities, bigotry, and immense discouragement, she pursued the dreams God placed in her heart. She influenced thousands of souls through her ministry. Pulpits may have been closed to Jarena Lee, but the God of Heaven softened the hearts of people so that He could fill them with His love. Society may have had a derogatory view of Jarena, but she did not let the opinions of others hinder her. Because of her resolve, this warrior overcame a prejudiced society to spread the love of Jesus.

## BENJAMIN BANNEKER—CHANGING THE WORLD WITH HIS MIND

*One universal Father hath given to us all . . . Endowed
us with the same faculties . . . We are all of the same
family.*

—FROM A LETTER TO THOMAS JEFFERSON, DATED AUGUST 19, 1791

Molly Walsh, though British and white, crossed the Atlantic as a slave. For the price of seven years of slavery, she exchanged her freedom for the opportunity of a better future in the Americas and immigrated as an indentured servant to the colony of Maryland. When her servitude ended, she purchased a farm near the Patapsco River, close to Baltimore. She purchased two slaves and, after setting them free, fell in love with and married one of them—a black man named Banneker.

One of their children, Mary Banneker, grew up, purchased a black slave named Robert, and married him. On October 9, 1731, they had a child who would change the world with his mind— Benjamin Banneker.

As Benjamin grew, it became clear that this young man was of superior intellectual ability. When he was just fifteen years of age, he designed an irrigation system that enabled the family farm to thrive, even in times of drought. He became proficient on the violin and the flute, and attained an eighth grade education—a huge achievement for a teenager at that time in the South.

A simple pocket watch changed his life forever. In 1753, at the age of twenty-two, Benjamin borrowed a pocket watch from a neighbor and proved that his intellect and ingenuity was far above average. He went home, took apart the borrowed timepiece, and sketched each component on paper. His drawing was so accurate that he actually counted the number of teeth on each gear and carefully calculated the relationship between each of them. Using his sketch, Benjamin was able to carve each component out of wood.

Once Benjamin Banneker built his clock, it struck every hour, on the hour, with total accuracy for over forty years. That amazing timepiece opened doors for this man to soar above every expectation for the son of slaves. He was unwilling to let his race or his age hinder him from developing mentally. Even considering his glorious achievements as a youth, an even greater accomplishment awaited him.

Benjamin Banneker met a renowned industrialist, Joseph Ellicott. Recognizing the intellectual capacity in the young man, Ellicott befriended Banneker and loaned him a collection of books. Through those books and additional independent study, he taught himself astronomy and mathematics. He predicted the solar eclipse that occurred on April 14, 1789. His prediction contradicted the most prominent scientists of his day, but on the day of reckoning, he was right.

In 1791 Benjamin caught the eye of then President George

Washington, who appointed him as part of a three-man team sent to survey the city that became Washington, D.C. He was the first black presidential appointee.

Benjamin Banneker, a black and a son of slaves, sent a letter of rebuke to one of the founding fathers of the United States. Mr. Thomas Jefferson was a known slaveholder who documented that blacks were mentally inferior. In response, Banneker sent him this letter of rebuke, as well as an almanac he had written, which was comparable to the best work of Benjamin Franklin. However, he became best known for the letter, in which he wrote:

> *Sir, how pitiable is it to reflect, that although you were so fully convinced of the benevolence of the Father of Mankind, and of his equal and impartial distribution of these rights and privileges, which he hath conferred upon them, that you should at the same time counteract his mercies, in detaining by fraud and violence so numerous a part of my brethren, under groaning captivity and cruel oppression, that you should at the same time be found guilty of that most criminal act, which you professedly detested in others, with respect to yourselves.*

The message cut deeply. The eloquence and the knowledge displayed in both the letter and the almanac shattered the racial stereotypes that had existed in Thomas Jefferson's mind for years. In response, Thomas Jefferson replied:

> *I can add with truth that nobody wishes more ardently*

*to see a good system commenced for raising the
condition of both their body & mind to what it ought to
be, as fast as the imbecillity of their present existence,
and other circumstances which cannot be neglected, will
admit. I have taken the liberty of sending your almanac
to Monsieur de Condorcet, Secretary of the Academy of
Sciences at Paris, and member of the Philanthropic
society because I considered it as a document to which
your whole colour had a right for their justification
against the doubts which have been entertained of them.
I am with great esteem, Sir, Your most obedt. humble
servt. Th. Jefferson*

Benjamin Banneker would go down in history as the man who
proved that blacks were not mentally inferior—not because of his
shouts of anger and protest, but with the proof of his life and his
relationship with God. His ability to stand firm despite the
intimidation that surrounded him was more than commendable. It
was honorable.

# OLD ELIZABETH—THE CONVERSION OF A CAPTIVE

At only eleven years old, the slave girl, Elizabeth, was sold to another farm several miles away from her parents and siblings. In agony over her sudden departure from the life she knew, she asked her new overseer if she could travel to see her mother at her former home. Her master denied her request. However, he underestimated the determination of this young girl. Without the knowledge of her overseer, she set off to walk twenty miles in order to reunite with her mother, whom she would likely never have seen again otherwise.

Elizabeth reached the estate where her mother labored as a slave, found her mother, and stayed with her for a few days. Yet she could not shake the lingering and inevitable realization that she would have to part with her mother and face the consequences of her secret departure from her captor's home. It was time to go back.

Sorrowfully, she began her journey to her master but not before her mother offered these simple words of comfort, "You have nobody in the wide world to look to but God."

These words fell upon young Elizabeth's heart so heavily that she repeated them all the way back to her new owners. Upon her arrival, this eleven-year-old girl was tied and beaten severely. Having "no one else but God," she gave herself to prayer from that moment on. Expressing only to Him the depths of her sorrow, she continually prayed, until she could grieve no further.

"Rise up and pray!"

The voice she heard in her misery suddenly strengthened her. She was able to gather enough strength to pray that God would have mercy upon her. Her account of what happened afterwards showed that God would not only have mercy on her, but would change her life forever.

> *Knowing no more to say, I halted, but continued on my knees. My spirit was then taught to pray, "Lord, have mercy on me—Christ, save me." Immediately there appeared a director, clothed in white raiment. I thought he took me by the hand and said, "Come with me." He led me down a long journey to a fiery gulf, and left me standing upon the brink of this awful pit.*

> *I began to scream for mercy, thinking I was about to be plunged to the belly of hell, and believed I should sink to endless ruin. Although I prayed and wrestled with all my might, it seemed in vain. Still, I felt all the while that I was sustained by some invisible power. At this solemn moment, I thought I saw a hand from which hung, as it were, a silver hair, and a voice told me that all the hope I had of being saved was no more than a hair; still, pray, and it will be sufficient.*

> *I then renewed my struggle, crying for mercy and salvation, until I found that every cry raised me higher and higher, and my head was quite above the fiery pillars. Then I thought I was permitted to look straight*

*forward, and saw the Saviour standing with His hand stretched out to receive me. An indescribably glorious light was in Him, and He said, "Peace, peace, come unto Me."*

*At this moment I felt that my sins were forgiven me, and the time of my deliverance was at hand. I sprang forward and fell at His feet, giving Him all the thanks and highest praises, crying, "Thou hast redeemed me— Thou hast redeemed me to Thyself." I felt filled with light and love.*

*At this moment I thought my former guide took me again by the hand and led me upward, till I came to the celestial world and to Heaven's door, which I saw was open, and while I stood there, a power surrounded me which drew me in, and I saw millions of glorified spirits in white robes. After I had this view, I thought I heard a voice saying, "Art thou willing to be saved?" I said, "Yes, Lord."*

*Again I was asked, "Art thou willing to be saved in My way?" I stood speechless until He asked me again, "Art thou willing to be saved in My way?" Then I heard a whispering voice say, "If thou art not saved in the Lord's way, thou canst not be saved at all;" at which I exclaimed, "Yes, Lord, in Thy own way." Immediately a light fell upon my head, and I was filled with light, and I was shown the world lying in wickedness, and was told I must go there, and call the people to repentance, for the day of the Lord was at hand; and this message was as a heavy yoke upon me, so that I wept bitterly at the thought of what I should have to pass through.*

*While I wept, I heard a voice say, "Weep not, some will laugh at thee, some will scoff at thee, and the dogs will bark at thee, but while thou doest My will, I will be with thee to the ends of the earth."*[5]

From this young slave girl's glorious conversion came a call to preach the gospel, which she did until her ninety-seventh year. History never tells us exactly how many lives she touched, neither does history seem to remember all of the mountains this servant of God overcame in order to finish her course. In this world, she saw Jesus face to face. She received the honor of serving Him for the remainder of her life. She was given the sacred trust of carrying the love of Jesus into a world where hatred reigned.

## HENRY BROWN—ESCAPED IN A BOX

Henry Brown's wife and children had just been sold to another master, leaving him alone, a slave without his family. Henry Brown was distraught, watching his family taken away in chains to a place where he would never again see them.

*The purchaser of my wife was a Methodist minister, who was about starting for North Carolina. Pretty soon five waggon-loads of little children passed, and looking at the foremost one, what should I see but a little child, pointing its tiny hand towards me, exclaiming, "There's my father; I knew he would come and bid me good-bye." It was my eldest child! Soon the gang approached in which my wife was chained. I looked, and beheld her familiar face; but O, reader, that glance of agony! May God spare me ever again enduring the excruciating horror of that moment! She passed, and came near to where I stood. I seized hold of her hand, intending to bid her farewell; but words failed me; the gift of utterance had fled, and I remained speechless. I followed her for some distance, with her hand grasped in mine, as if to save her from her fate, but I could not speak, and I was obliged to turn away in silence.[6]*

Comparatively, Henry's life as a slave was not as bad as the unfortunate tortures that many of his fellow slaves had endured. But the loss of his family demoralized him, and as far as he was concerned, it was all that could be tolerated.

> *But I did not waste my precious furlough in idle*
> *mourning over my fate. I armed myself with determined*
> *energy, for action, and in the words of one of old, in the*
> *name of God, "I leaped over a wall, and run through a*
> *troop" of difficulties. After searching for assistance for*
> *some time, I at length was so fortunate as to find a*
> *friend, who promised to assist me, for one half the money*
> *I had about me, which was one hundred and sixty-six*
> *dollars. I gave him eighty-six, and he was to do his best*
> *in forwarding my scheme. Long did we remain together,*
> *attempting to devise ways and means to carry me away*
> *from the land of separation of families, of whips and*
> *thumbscrews, and auction blocks; but as often as a plan*
> *was suggested by my friend, there would appear some*
> *difficulty in the way of its accomplishment. Perhaps it*
> *may not be best to mention what these plans were, as*
> *some unfortunate slaves may thereby be prevented from*
> *availing themselves of these methods of escape.*
>
> *At length, after praying earnestly to Him, who seeth afar*
> *off, for assistance, in my difficulty, suddenly, as if from*
> *above, there darted into my mind these words, "Go and*
> *get a box, and put yourself in it." I pondered the words*
> *over in my mind. "Get a box?" thought I, "What can this*
> *mean?" But I was "not disobedient unto the heavenly*
> *vision," and I determined to put into practice this*
> *direction, as I considered it, from my heavenly Father.*[7]

Henry longed for freedom—to the point where he would ship himself up North, in a three-foot by two-foot box.

*I went to the depot, and there noticed the size of the largest boxes, which commonly were sent by the cars, and returned with their dimensions. I then repaired to a carpenter, and induced him to make me a box of such a description as I wished, informing him of the use I intended to make of it. He assured me I could not live in it; but as it was dear liberty I was in pursuit of, I thought it best to make the trial.*

*When the box was finished, I carried it, and placed it before my friend, who had promised to assist me, who asked me if that was to "put my clothes in." I replied that it was not, but to "put Henry Brown in!" He was astonished at my temerity; but I insisted upon his placing me in it, and nailing me up, and he finally consented.*

*After corresponding with a friend in Philadelphia, arrangements were made for my departure, and I took my place in this narrow prison, with a mind full of uncertainty as to the result. It was a critical period of my life, I can assure you, reader; but if you have never been deprived of your liberty, as I was, you cannot realize the power of that hope of freedom, which was to me indeed, "an anchor to the soul, both sure and steadfast."*

*I laid me down in my darkened home of three feet by two, and like one about to be guillotined, resigned myself* to my fate. My friend was to accompany me, but he failed to do so; and contented himself with sending a telegraph message to his correspondent in Philadelphia, that such a box was on its way to his care.

I started with my head downwards, although the box was directed, "this side up with care." From the express office, I was carried to the depot, and from thence tumbled roughly into the baggage car, where I happened to fall "right side up," but no thanks to my transporters. But after a while the cars stopped, and I was put aboard a steamboat, and placed on my head. In this dreadful position, I remained the space of an hour and a half, it seemed to me, when I began to feel of my eyes and head, and found to my dismay, that my eyes were almost swollen out of their sockets, and the veins on my temple seemed ready to burst. I made no noise however, determining to obtain "victory or death," but endured the terrible pain, as well as I could, sustained under the whole by the thoughts of sweet liberty. About half an hour afterwards, I attempted again to lift my hands to my face, but I found I was not able to move them. A cold sweat now covered me from head to foot. Death seemed my inevitable fate, and every moment I expected to feel the blood flowing over me, which had burst from my veins. One half hour longer and my sufferings would have ended in that fate, which I preferred to slavery; but I lifted up my heart to God in prayer, believing that he would yet deliver me, when to my joy, I overheard two men say, "We have been here two hours and have travelled twenty miles, now let us sit down, and rest ourselves." They suited the action to the word, and turned the box over, containing my soul and body, thus delivering me from the power of the grim messenger of death, who a few moments previously, had aimed his fatal shaft at my head, and had placed his icy hands on my throbbing heart. One of these men inquired of the other, what he supposed that box contained, to which his comrade replied, that he guessed it was the mail. "Yes," thought I, "it is a male, indeed, although not the mail of the United States."

Soon after this fortunate event, we arrived at Washington, where I was thrown from the wagon, and again as my luck would have it, fell on my head. I was then rolled down a declivity, until I reached the platform from which the cars were to start. During this short but rapid journey, my neck came very near being dislocated, as I felt it crack, as if it had snapped asunder. Pretty soon, I heard someone say, "there is no room for this box, it will have to remain behind." I then again applied to the Lord, my help in all my difficulties, and in a few minutes I heard a gentleman direct the hands to place it aboard, as "it came with the mail and must go on with it." I was then tumbled into the car, my head downwards again, as I seemed to be destined to escape on my head; a sign probably, of the opinion of American people respecting such bold adventurers as myself; that our heads should be held downwards, whenever we attempt to benefit ourselves. Not the only instance of this *propensity, on the part of the American people, towards the colored race. We had not proceeded far, however, before more baggage was placed in the car, at a stopping place, and I was again turned to my proper position. No farther difficulty occurred until my arrival at Philadelphia. I reached this place at three o'clock in the morning, and remained in the depot until six o'clock, A. M., at which time, a waggon drove up, and a person inquired for a box directed to such a place, "right side up." I was soon placed on this waggon, and carried to the house of my friend's correspondent, where quite a number of persons were waiting to receive me. They appeared to be some afraid to open the box at first, but at length one of them rapped upon it, and with a trembling voice, asked, "Is all right within?" to which I replied, "All right." The joy of these friends was excessive, and like the ancient Jews, who repaired to the rebuilding of Jerusalem, each one seized hold of some tool, and commenced opening my grave. At length the cover was removed, and I arose, and shook myself from the lethargy into which I had fallen; but exhausted nature proved too much for my frame, and I swooned away.*[8]

Henry Brown escaped to freedom's arms, arriving in Philadelphia. Through listening to the voice of God, he was able to remain free for the rest of his life. It is certain that Henry Brown is in the arms of God, and forever again united with his family.

## JOHN MARRANT—THE STORM STOPPER

Born as a free black in 1775, a year before the Declaration of Independence was signed, John Marrant's life is a triumph in more ways than one. All odds seemed against him growing up. His father died when John was very young. America was a country with a huge racial divide and little opportunity for young black children, whether they were free or slave. But Marrant had an uncanny ability to seize opportunities, no matter what odds he faced.

Before Marrant was a teenager, he learned to play two different instruments—the French horn and the violin. He was so skilled that he was often invited to social gatherings to play his beautiful music for many important socialites of his day.

On one of his increasingly routine outings as a young teenager Marrant had intended to stir trouble in the gathering of men and women. But a preacher by the name of George Whitefield spoke a stirring message that penetrated the heart of this young musician. So powerful was the message that Marrant fell to his face for over a half-hour upon hearing it. Soon after his conversion, he gave himself to Bible study and prayer.

While his conversion was glorious, his family's response was less than glorious. They accused him of insanity, calling his behavior bizarre. They began to unjustly persecute him because of his Christianity. In time, he voluntarily exiled himself from his place of residence and began to live life as a wanderer until he crossed paths with a Native American, who embraced him fully and allowed him to reside with his people, the Cherokees.

Among the Cherokees Marrant became an evangelist, preaching the gospel every chance he could. Many souls came to Christ through his ministry, and many lasting bonds were created between blacks and Cherokees from the passion that this young man had for Christ's message. His story began at fifteen years old, when Marrant, after deserting his family, was captured by the Cherokee Indians and sentenced to execution for entering their land. It was the following experience that prompted Marrant's mission to reach the indigenous people of America with the saving message of God's love.

> *There was an Indian fortification all round the town, and a guard placed at each entrance. The hunter [a Cherokee hunter Marrant met in the woods] passed one of these without molestation, but I was stopped by the guard and examined. They asked me where I came from, and what was my business there. My companion of the woods attempted to speak for me, but was not permitted; he was taken away, and I saw him no more. I was now surrounded by about 50 men, and carried to one of their chiefs to be examined by him. When I came before him, he asked me what was my business there. I told him I came there with a hunter, whom I met with in the woods. He replied, "Did I not know that whoever came there 'without giving a better account of themselves' than I did, was to be put to death?" I said I did not know it.*

*Observing that I answered him so readily in his own language, he asked me where I learnt it. To this I returned no answer, but burst out into a flood of tears; and calling upon my Lord Jesus.*

*At this he stood astonished, and expressed a concern for me, and said I was young. He asked me who my Lord Jesus was. To this I gave him no answer, but continued praying and weeping. Addressing himself to the officer who stood by him, he said he was sorry; but it was the law, and it must not be broken. I was then ordered to be taken away, and put into a place of confinement. They led me from their court into a low dark place, and thrust me into it, very dreary and dismal; they made fast the door, and set a watch. The judge sent for the executioner, and gave him his warrant for my execution in the afternoon of the next day. The executioner came, and gave me notice of it, which made me very happy, as the near prospect of death made me hope for a speedy deliverance from the body: And truly this dungeon became my chapel, for the Lord Jesus did not leave me in this great trouble, but was very present, so that I continued blessing Him, and singing His praises all night without ceasing: The watch hearing the noise, informed the executioner that somebody had been in the dungeon with me all night; upon which he came in to see and to examine, with a great torch lighted in his hand, who it was I had with me; but finding nobody, he turned round, and asked me who it was? I told him it was the Lord Jesus Christ; but he made no answer, turned away, went out, and locked my door. At the hour appointed for my execution I was taken out, and led to the destined spot, amidst a vast number of people. I praised the Lord all the way we went, and when we arrived at the place I understood the kind of death I was to suffer, yet, blessed be God, none of those things moved me. The executioner shewed me a basket of turpentine wood, stuck full of small pieces, like skewed; he told me I was to be stripped naked, and laid down in the basket, and these sharp pegs were to be stuck into me, and then set on fire, and when they had burnt to my body, I was to be turned on the other side, and served in the same manner, and then to be taken by four men and thrown into the flame, which was to finish the execution. I burst into tears, and asked what I had done to deserve so cruel a death! To this he gave me no answer. I cried out, Lord, if it be Thy will that it should be so, Thy will be done: I then asked the executioner to let me go to prayer; he asked me to whom? I answered, to the Lord my God; he seemed surprised, and asked me where he was? I told him he was present; upon which he gave me leave. I desired them all to do as I did, so I fell down upon my knees, and mentioned to the Lord his delivering of the three children in the fiery furnace, and of Daniel in the lions' den, and had close communion with God. I prayed in English a considerable time, and about the middle of my prayer, the Lord impressed a strong desire upon my mind to turn into their language, and pray in their tongue. I did so, and with remarkable liberty, which wonderfully affected the people. One circumstance was very singular, and strikingly displays the power and grace of God. I believe the executioner was savingly converted to God. He rose from his knees, and embraced me round the middle, and was unable to speak for about five minutes; the first words he expressed, when he had utterance, were, "No man shall hurt thee till thou hast been to the king."*[9]

In the king's presence, the Lord had made his enemies his friends. Miraculously, his sentence of death was acquitted, due to the constant and tearful persuasion of the very men who were to carry out his execution. Once freed, he continued his ministry among the Native Americans, with great success.

God turned John Marrant's enemies into friends, and He can certainly accomplish this seemingly impossible feat with anyone who will trust in Him. His faithfulness, even in the face of adverity, was proven once again in the life of Marrant. And God, to this very day, remains in the business of reconciling enemies into friends.[10]

# David George—Preaching Across Racial Lines

> *The Ministers were not allowed to come amongst us lest*
> *they should furnish us with too much knowledge."*

David George was born a slave in Virginia. He spent most of his childhood years as a fieldworker in Essex County. In his childhood, a particular act of cruelty drove him to flee from his slave master and not look back.

His last view of his mother was her kneeling frame, begging for mercy as a group of young men stripped and whipped her until she nearly died. David never knew if she lived or died, as he fled the plantation soon after. He was recaptured by an Indian chief who kept him as a slave, but according to David, he was treated kindly in all his labors.

When his original slave master followed his tracks and prepared to purchase him back from the Indian chief, David escaped again. He fled to dwell among another Indian tribe called the Natchee Indians.

While he lived among this tribe he was told plainly by a black man who went by the name Cyrus that if he did not take serious consideration of his soul, he would not see the face of God in glory. Whatever became of Cyrus is unknown, but his simple message changed David's life. His years of slavery paled in comparison to the eternal helplessness he felt in never seeing the One who placed him on this earth. His menial accomplishments in life became even more menial. His failures were reduced to nothing, compared to his consistent denial of the great salvation of God, through Jesus Christ.

David George sought God, but he also met someone who could help him grow in his faith. He soon began to hear the preaching ministry of a man named George Liele, who greatly influenced his commitment to God. To say that David George grew would be an understatement—the spiritual impact he had on countless lives is remembered in heaven today. He became an effective preacher and began his ministry in earnest. Then, one day, he was sought out by congregates who turned out to be unexpected but welcome guests to George's all-black congregation.

> *Mr. William Taylor and his wife, two [white] Baptists, who came from London to Shelburne, heard of me. She came to my house when I was so poor that I had no money to buy any potatoes for feed, and was so good as to give my children somewhat, and me, money enough to buy a bushel of potatoes; which one produced thirty five (35) bushels. The church was now grown to about fifty (50) members. At this time a white person, William Holmes, who, with Deborah, his wife, had been converted by reading the scriptures, and lived at Jones Harbour, about twenty (20) miles down the river, came up for me, and would have me go away with him in his schooner to his house, I went with him, first to his house, and then to a town they called Liverpool, inhabited by*

*white people. Many had been baptized there by Mr.*
*Chippenham, of Annapolis in N. S. Mr. Jesse Dexter*
*preached to them, but was not their pastor. His was a*
*mixed communion church, I preached there; the*
*Christians were all alive, and we had a little heaven*
*together. We then returned to Brother Holmes and he*
*and his wife came up with me to Shelburne, and gave*
*their experiences to the church on Thursday, and were*
*baptized on Lord's day. Their relations who lived in the*
*town were very angry, raised a mob, and endeavoured to*
*hinder their being baptized.*

*The persecution increased, and became so great, that it*
*did not seem possible to preach, and I thought I must*
*leave Shelburne. Several of the black people had houses*
*upon my lot, but forty (40) or fifty (50) disbanded*
*soldiers were employed, who came with the tackle of*
*ships, and turned my dwelling house, and every one of*
*their houses, quite over, and the meeting house they*
*would have burned down, had not the ringleader of the*
*mob himself prevented it . . . . But I continued to*
*preaching.*[11]

"I continued to preaching." How much resolve does it take to
stay your course when your very life is in danger? How great can a
person's bravery be, that he can disregard his own safety for the
faith on which he or she stands? David George was one of those
greats. His life was the definition of true freedom—the freedom to

be who God desires. He was one of the brave souls who did not run when the fires of persecution came roaring towards him. This Godly man continued to do what God had called him to do. The most overwhelming circumstances turned this once fearful man into a soldier for Christ.[12]

## MOSES WILKINSON—UNSUNG HERO

Moses Wilkinson stood at the pulpit with a fiery look in his
eye. His voice boomed from one end of the church to the other. The
members of the Methodist Church in Birchtown stood in awe of the
power that came forth from this man, who was unlike most
preachers.

The fact that Old Moses was a fiery, influential preacher was
not his most outstanding quality. Moses was blind, crippled, unable
to work a regular job, and the pastor of the largest church in
Birchtown. He was being supported every day by an unknown
donor.

Moses Wilkinson was at a clear disadvantage in his day.
Racial issues coupled with the fact that he was crippled and blind
could easily have broken the will of this simple man. He could have
resolved to live in dependence on others and retreated from anything
resembling vision, integrity, or character. Instead, the ministry of
the gospel became his life's calling. He fulfilled this calling with
more impact than many who had eyes to see and legs to walk.

Wilkinson's church became the most important gathering place
in the community. It became a center for security and political
discussion—pastored by a man who mastered overwhelming
obstacles that stood against him every day of his life.

Though weak in appearance, through tremendous spiritual
strength, Old Moses lived a life of humility and service that made

him a spiritual giant to all who heard his message of God's truth.

Old Moses' church was soon the largest church in his city—so influential that his first convert was Peggy King. Her husband, Boston, was a faithless dissenter, until the love of God also came into his heart.

Moses' blindness and crippling did not stop him from becoming who he was called to be. He was so fiery a preacher that many feared for his health as he preached with a fervency that could match that of any healthy young man. He went above and beyond the expectation of a blind, crippled man.

Moses Wilkinson was an unsung hero of the church. And although he may not have chapters in the history books, his converts did. The great preacher and missionary to Africa, Boston King, was one of them.

# BOSTON KING—THE RELUCTANT MISSIONARY

With an opportunity from his slave master to apprentice as a carpenter, the young slave, Boston King, did not experience an atmosphere in which to learn. The only black apprentice among his peers, he shouldered the blame for lost tools and mistakes around the shop. And when tools, or even nails, were thought to be lost or stolen, young Boston was beaten without mercy by the shop owners to the point he could not work for weeks.

When the news of such beatings reached the ears of Boston's slave master, he intervened, not because he cared about Boston, but because Boston was his property, and the slave master could not afford for him to be permanently damaged by the shop owner. This intervention was effective, and Boston was able to properly gain knowledge of his trade. However, his slave master would never benefit from his service as a carpenter because Boston fled from his captivity not long after returning to his master.

Boston King ran into the hands of the English Army, who received him gladly and treated him humanely in the face of the American Revolution. He, along with his comrades, was infected with smallpox. He had to be removed a mile from camp and could no longer march with the British Army.

Through miraculous provision and a Godly relief worker, Boston eventually recovered from his affliction. Not long after this, his wife became the first convert of the great orator, Moses

Wilkinson. Her conversion was so dramatic that Boston's heart became troubled. One could only imagine what went through his mind. Perhaps it was a dream that he had as a child:

*When [I was] 12 years old, it pleased God to alarm me by a remarkable dream. At midday, when the cattle went under the shade of the trees, I dreamt that the world was on fire, and that I saw the supreme Judge defend on His great white Throne. I saw millions of millions of souls; some of whom ascended up to heaven; while others were rejected, and fell into the greatest confusion and despair. This dream made such an impression upon my mind, that I refrained from swearing and bad company, and from that time acknowledged that there was a God; but how to serve God I knew not.* [13]

His lack of knowledge did not last forever. Soon after his wife's conversion, God dealt powerfully with Boston King, but King began to resist God's dealing and fell into doubt and depression. Then one day, God began to speak to him.

*I continued in prayer about half an hour, when the Lord . . . spoke to my heart, "Peace be unto thee." All my doubts and fears vanished away: I saw, but faith, heaven opened to my view; and Christ and His holy angels rejoicing over me. I was now enabled to believe in the name of Jesus, and my Soul was dissolved into love. Everything appeared to me in a different light to what they did before; and loved every living creature upon the*

*face of the earth. I could truly say, I was now become a*
*new creature. All tormenting and slavish fear, and all*
*the guilt and weight of sin were done away. I was so*
*exceedingly blessed, that I could no longer conceal my*
*happiness, but went to my brethren and told them what*
*the Lord had done for my soul.*[14]

Soon after this miraculous experience, Boston began to experience a burden for the lost. He gave his life to serving God and soon became one of the most influential missionaries to Africa. He was one of the first black Americans to leave America and travel to Africa to preach the gospel.

Boston King's life was one of supernatural communication with God. Although, like all of us, he faced doubts and fears, his conversations with God included not only talking, but also listening. Because he listened, his impact crossed the natural borders of oceans and touched the lives of lost human beings.

# HENRY GARNETT—THE SLAVE WHO CAUGHT THE EAR OF CONGRESS

Thanks to the generosity and outright bravery of a family of Quakers, the young Garnett family was able to escape the brutality of slavery and wander northward in constant hiding. Eventually, they reached New York, where young Henry pursued an education. Despite his education, he could not find work and went to sea seeking a livelihood.

On his return trip to shore, he found his former place of residence destroyed. He discovered the worst had happened—his home had been raided by slave hunters, and his sister taken captive. His father was able to escape the imminent danger by jumping from a second floor window out of the sight of his would-be captors.

Furious and bent on revenge, Henry Garnett began to hunt those who had captured his family. He certainly would have continued, if his friends had not convinced him to lay low. He submitted to their pleading and stopped his rampage. This was only the beginning of his challenges.

Henry, along with a group of other black students, was admitted into a school in the free state of New Hampshire. On Independence Day those students began to speak out against the horrors of slavery, and demanded abolition of this institution. This act angered the locals, and in response to the students' words, they destroyed and dragged their entire schoolhouse into a swamp.

Henry and the group with him fled.

Henry's radicalism crossed the line of decency in the minds of black leaders of his day. Henry believed that slaves should rise up and slay their masters. He declared this viewpoint during a speech in 1843, which caused his influence upon the abolitionists of the day to decline.[15]

In the years to come, through much study, Henry became a minister of the gospel. In 1865, all that his life had endured reached a pinnacle. There he stood at the invitation of President Lincoln, in the chambers of the United States House of Representatives to deliver a message. His radicalism had become non-violent. The former slave had risen to the thrones of power in his nation to speak the heart of God. His message cut directly to the heart of the institution he so greatly abhorred:

> *Henry compared those who kept slaves to the Pharisees whom Jesus charged with laying heavy burdens on others while refusing to lift a finger themselves. He exclaimed, "Great God! I would as soon attempt to enslave Gabriel or Michael as to enslave a man made in the image of God, and for whom Christ died. Slavery is snatching man from the high place to which he was lifted by the hand of God, and dragging him down to the level of the brute creation, where he is made to be the companion of the horse and the fellow of the ox."*[16]

His passion for those enslaved was so great that he went to

Europe and organized a worldwide ban on cotton, feeling that in doing so, it would render the institution of slavery powerless. Henry was right. But the world did not follow suit. Still, Henry Garnett finished his race.[17]

Henry Garnett continued his life as a Presbyterian pastor and eventually journeyed to Africa as a missionary. Two months after his arrival in Africa, Henry went home to meet his Lord. Despite misguided passion, and being victimized by a system he abhorred, Henry Garnett opened the eyes of many leaders of his day, particularly after his death.

This man of war became a man who met with the Prince of Peace. His salvation did not render him powerless and weak but enabled him to fulfill his purpose God's way.

## DANIEL COKER—FIRST BLACK AMERICAN MISSIONARY TO AFRICA

Multiple churches in Sierra Leone and Liberia were founded by a black man. Although both of these nations are in West Africa, the man who founded the churches was born a slave in the United States.

In 1820, Daniel Coker was sent away from the only home he knew to reach lost souls a world away. There is far more to his story than this courageous journey across the seas.

Daniel was born in Maryland around 1780 and given the name Isaac Wright. His father was a slave born in Africa. His mother was a white indentured servant named Susan Coker. Such a reversal in parentage for a mixed child was unusual in that day. His mixed race brought him the opportunity to follow his white half-brothers to school, but only as a servant; yet he learned to read and write. Still a young man, he managed to flee slavery by escaping to New York where he changed his name to Daniel Coker.

This name change helped him avoid capture as a fugitive when he returned to the south. He met Bishop Francis Asbury who ordained him to the ministry. Through ordination his freedom from slavery was purchased. Daniel was no longer a fugitive, and his fear of living a life in chains was over.

Despite his ordination in the Methodist church, he still faced much discrimination. Daniel began to speak out for an independent black church that was unique and separate from the Methodists. In 1816, his prayers were answered.

The Reverend Richard Allen called a conference in Baltimore, Maryland. Reverend Allen, along with ministers from numerous churches, formed the African Methodist Episcopal Church. Daniel, working as the conference secretary, was elected as the denomination's first bishop. Even here, race was a factor for Daniel. Judged once again by the color of his skin, Daniel faced opposition because he was very fair-skinned. While it is not entirely known why he declined the election, many believe it was for this reason. Richard Allen was elected in his place.

Still, the formation of the AME Church was a welcome answer to prayer for this young minister. As a cofounder of the AME Church, he established schools and churches in the Baltimore area. He then went to Africa in the year 1820, funded by the American Colonization Society. There he founded numerous churches and left his mark on the dark continent. Again, his race was a factor in his ability to be effective. Daniel Coker was prohibited from a position of authority in the white-run society of Sierra Leone. Still, he continued his work in Africa for nearly three decades.

This slave-born man managed to cross the world with the gospel and cofound one of the largest African-American denominations. To this day the AME church thrives, thanks to the inspired leadership of a man who would not allow prejudice to keep him from following his dream.

Daniel Coker died in 1846, while serving God in Freetown, Sierra Leone. His determination made him the very first African American, born a slave, to travel back to Africa as a missionary.

———◦◦◦———

# LUCY SMITH—THE HEALING PREACHER

*Yes, I built this church seven years ago. It's the only church in Chicago built by a woman.*

—LUCY SMITH

The small room was all that was available, but it would have to do. People from all over came to visit the home of Lucy Smith. She was a woman of prayer, and they were a group of people with immense needs. One after the other, the reports came in—reports of healing and answered prayers. This consistent ministry continued for ten years, when it was decided to bring this prayer meeting out of the house and into a new church building.

The ministry that came out of the construction of this new church building was finally able to thrive. People came—whites, blacks, Europeans, and even Jews packed into the newly built edifice to worship God and received answers to their prayers—specifically healing.

Elder Lucy Smith was a servant to all people. She was a single black woman who was a senior pastor in the church. Such a situation was unthinkable in the 1920s. Yet, the power of criticism meant little when people of all races, by their own testimony, walked out of her church healed of illnesses, fed, and clothed—all by a black woman who built a church building from the ground up in the middle of Chicago.

God used the simplicity and sincerity of Elder Lucy Smith to touch many for the Kingdom of God. Elder Smith was born on a plantation in Woodstock, Georgia. She never saw her father and was raised by her mother. They were very poor and lived in a small cabin, no bigger than the podium of the church she eventually built.

She was married in 1896, but her husband left her to raise nine children alone. Hidden within the success story of her ministry is perhaps her greatest achievement, in that she succeeded in raising those children by working hard and trusting in God to take care of them.

Around the age of forty-two, she received her calling in the ministry of healing. She started the prayer meeting in her small home, which reached nations. From that one little spot her ministry reached the world.

In the years that followed, a church was built, and people were encouraged. Elder Smith preached all over the South and West of the United States, taking God's healing to hundreds. She glorified God in all that she did, and God blessed her efforts by increasing her ministry. Her influence spread from those who could fit inside her small home to an entire nation and even the world.

## MONTROSE WAITE—THE GREAT COMMISSION FOR WHITES ONLY

With great anticipation, the twenty-five-year-old minister, Montrose Waite, set off for the missions office where he could possibly be sent to his motherland to preach the gospel to his beloved people. But there appeared an ominous and hateful declaration that would attempt to crush his dreams and hinder his high calling. As he approached the missions office, he saw a sign hung on the front door—Whites Only.

This sign became the norm at nearly every missions organization he entered. But in February of 1922, his breakthrough came. The missions board from the still-young denomination, the Christian and Missionary Alliance, sent him a letter inviting him to go to Africa as a missionary. After his first trip, which lasted fourteen years, he was not invited to return to Africa because of the stiff opposition from many ministers who did not want a black missionary as part of their team.

In response to this, and through much discouragement and hardship, he and his wife founded the Afro-American Missionary Crusade (AAMC). Through this organization, he and his entire family went back to the nation of Sierra Leone in Africa in 1948—twelve years later.

Montrose continued serving God in Africa until 1962, at which time he returned to the United States. For Montrose Waite, the passion to preach the gospel to the souls in Africa was not a "Whites Only" issue. Souls were at stake. A burning passion to do the will of God was at stake. These convictions ran deeper than the color line, and the life of this man of God proved it. There is no way to count exactly how many souls he reached, but the great commission was for Montrose. He answered the call of Christ, rather than the oppression of man. He continued serving God until his death in 1977, and to this day, he is remembered as an apostle of missions to Africa.[18]

# WILLIAM SHEPPARD—CONFRONTING THE KING

With his surprising speed and foot-long teeth, the large hippopotamus lashed out at William Sheppard. Narrowly escaping the attack, this respected hunter and adventurer downed the giant animal with the crack of his rifle. With this fatal gunshot, he provided food for the hungry Congolese villagers.

William Sheppard, a Presbyterian missionary and adventurer in Africa, was born of slaves in 1865. As a preteen, William had heard about Africa and boldly stated, "When I grow up, I shall go there." However, for a black man born only three years after the Emancipation Proclamation was signed, it was clear that such opportunities would not come easily.

William served as a stable boy for a dentist in Virginia, where he was treated as a foster son. In this nurturing environment he learned to read. At the age of sixteen, he entered the school founded by Booker T. Washington, Hampton Institute. Upon completion, he entered seminary and subsequently found a job as a local minister. Finding his new job uninspiring, he began looking back at a childhood dream that still rested in his memory—Africa.

He approached the church board about going to the home of his ancestors as a missionary, but sadly, the answer was a stern "no." Then after an appeal to the denominational board, he was allowed to go under one condition—that he be accompanied by a white minister.

Samuel Lapsley accompanied William Sheppard, and although his desire was sincere, their relationship seemed to be more of a servant-master relationship until they arrived on the African continent, where the tables turned. William Sheppard proved to be far more skilled at roughing the African terrain and relating to the natives.

The two men began to blaze a trail through Africa in order to reach a hidden and elusive tribe called the Kubas. The Kubas were genuinely drawn to the charisma of Sheppard and decided not to kill him, which was their custom with intruders. Lapsley, on the other hand, became disheartened and discouraged about his role there. In comparison with Sheppard, he was more like a sidekick or servant, and certainly not the man in charge. Though genuine in his efforts, Lapsely was unable to endure this difficult and treacherous journey. He died two years later of blackwater fever.

Sheppard continued on and was able to accomplish much among the Kuba tribe. He even called his wife from America to join him. Together, they established a thriving mission staffed exclusively by Africans.

As the mission thrived, the church decided that Sheppard's former comrade, Lapsley, needed to be replaced. They sent a reporter named William Morrison, and the challenge of Sheppard's life began.

Morrison used the missionary label for his own agenda, which he deliberately pulled the reluctant Sheppard into. Morrison's agenda was to expose the deeds of the Belgian king, Leopold.

Working with rival tribes, King Leopold persecuted and massacred the indigenous people, with the intent to force them into slave labor. Sheppard received notice of these atrocities when he happened upon mutilated corpses lying in a field. He counted each corpse one by one, including a pile of hands severed by the colonizers, to ensure that the deeds had been done. Upon his arrival in the United States, Sheppard widely publicized the deeds of King Leopold and gained the reputation of a human rights crusader. These actions gained him much adoration in the United States, in a time when racial tensions were thick.

William Sheppard's mission to Africa ended, but his years in Africa were an adventure that earned him the name "Black Livingstone," after the great missionary David Livingstone.

The desire and vision of his life was realized. He went to Africa and changed lives through his service to God and his drive to overcome all obstacles before him in order to do the impossible. He became the slave who confronted the king.

⸙

## CUDJO LEWIS—LAST SLAVE STANDING

After more than 300 years of slavery ended, there was one man remaining who had actually been born in the motherland of Africa. Before his death in 1935, Cudjo Lewis described his capture:

*The tribes of Africa were engaged in civil war, and the prevailing tribes sold the members of the conquered tribes into slavery. The village of the Tarkbar tribe near the city of Tamale was raided by Dahomey warriors, and the survivors of the raid were taken to Whydah, now the People's Republic of Benin, and put up for sale. The captured tribesmen were sold for $100 each at Whydah. They were taken to the United States on board the schooner* Clotilde, *under the command of Maine Capt. William Foster. Foster had been hired by Capt. Timothy Meaher, a wealthy Mobile shipper and shipyard owner, who had built the schooner* Clotilde *in Mobile in 1856.* [19]

At the time of his capture, the import of African slaves to the United States was illegal. As they crossed the ocean, the United States government waited for them. All the slaveholders were acquitted of this crime against humanity after their arrest and trial. Many believe that the start of the Civil War was the reason for the acquittal. Those who had been carried as cargo on the ship were sold as slaves in a place that was known as AfricaTown.

*AfricaTown is unique in that it represents a group of*

*Africans who were forcefully removed from their
homeland, sold into slavery, and then formed their own,
largely self-governing community, all the while
maintaining a strong sense of African cultural heritage.
This sense of heritage and sense of community continues
to thrive today, more than 140 years after the landing of
the* Clotilde *in Mobile Bay.*[20]

The last slave standing, Cudjo lived beyond the Civil War and
into the 20th Century. Though he lived without his freedom, he did
not die in chains. He died as a man who was free in Jesus Christ, as
described shortly before Cudjo's death:

*Upon graduation from college in 1933, I went directly to
Mobile, Alabama, to begin my ministry of evangelism.
Upon my arrival, one of my dearest friends, who had
graduated earlier and now lived there, wanted to show
me the sights.*

*He asked if I had seen Cudjo. I asked, "What is that?"
He answered, "Cudjo is not a what but a who." I then
inquired, "Who is that?"*

*My friend explained that Cudjo was the only black man
still living who had crossed the ocean on a slave boat.*

*I assured my friend that I wanted to see this man, so we
drove out to his little cabin situated on a little knoll just
outside the city limits. As we approached, we could see
Cudjo sitting on the porch, rocking. He stood up as we*

*approached. With a big smile on his face, he assured us we were welcome. He was a stately man with hair and beard as white as snow.*

*After a long visit, we prepared to leave. I asked Cudjo if he was saved. He assured me that he was, and I asked him how he knew. He said he was a good man. I assured him that he could be a good man and not be saved.*

*He replied, "Oh, the preacher wants me to tell him why I know I'm saved."*

*"Yes," I said, "that is what I want to know: how do you know you are saved?"*

*He said, "Cudjo show you why he know." He looked around until he found a little piece of string; then taking a handkerchief out of his pocket he held it up and tried to push the string through it. He looked at my friend and said, "Can you push string through handkerchief?" My friend assured him he couldn't. . . He looked at me, and I shook my head. Then he said, "President of United States, biggest man in world, smartest man in world, he can't push it through!" We assured him that the President couldn't do it either. Then he said, "Cudjo can push it through." We asked him how he would do it. He said, "Cudjo get a needle. He put string in needle. He push needle through and string come through with it."*

*Then his eyes filled with tears as he lifted his face toward Heaven. As I looked into that tear-stained face, I felt I*

had never seen a man closer to God than old Cudjo
Lewis, over a hundred years old, the last living slave who
crossed the ocean on a slave boat. He said, "Jesus is the
Needle; Cudjo is the string; Cudjo is in Jesus, and when
Jesus goes through He take Cudjo through."

I said, "Praise God! If I live to be a thousand years old,
I will never hear it any plainer than that."[21]

## PETER CLAVER—A SLAVE TO THE SLAVES

In the humid air, the smell of decay traveled up the shores of Cartenga and touched the compassionate soul of Peter Claver. It was the scent of death and bondage that told him service was needed.

Peter Claver was unable to stop the slave trade, but he knew in his heart he could somehow serve those being sold into slavery. He traveled to Cartenga in 1610 and appointed himself as "slave to the Negroes forever." Claver was of African descent. The tropical climate in the northern part of South America was beautiful to some, but to those arriving in bondage on a ship, it was the destination where their deepest sorrows were realized—the port where their lives as slaves would begin.

After a two-month journey from West Africa, the ships emptied their cargo of men, woman, and children. At least a third of them arrived dead. Those still alive were greeted by one who looked like their brother, yet represented Christ in this new world.

With the arrival of a slave ship, Claver's eyes would light up at the chance to minister to and baptize the fearful and suffering individuals. The smells of slave ships—human defecation, dead bodies, and blood—kept others away. But in Peter Claver's eyes each small cell contained a soul who despertately needed the love of Jesus.

First he provided them with medical care, food, and cleansing.

"We must," Claver believed, "speak to them with our hands before we try to speak to them with our lips."

Claver prepared himself for his day's work by first praying and then passing through the streets of Cartenga with a cross placed high upon his staff. He took with him food, clothing, and other necessities for those he was committed to. He cared for the sick first. Then he taught them using drawings and illustrations of the passion of Christ.

As often as he could, he would impart the Word of God to those who were enslaved. With a life of servitude and suffering ahead of them, it was certain that many of them would experience life everlasting because of Claver's obedience to God.

Some say that Father Claver radiated the light of God when he ministered to these African souls. He did not, like so many others, minister to them from a distance. He walked among them and served them as if he were a slave born to serve them. He shone upon them the compassion that only Christ could offer a soul who suffered so greatly. He would lie there with them, in the dirt and defecation, knowing that he himself risked disease and even hostility. Yet those threats did not stop him from fulfilling his mission.

Claver often ministered to those who were dying. He shared with them the love of Jesus and begged of them to turn from their sins and embrace the cross. This they did by the thousands—one soul at a time.

Miraculously, Claver found favor with the slave drivers, illustrating the truth of the scripture, "When a man's ways please the Lord, even his enemies are at peace with him."

Sometimes, an African man or woman would be so replete with sores that bystanders could hardly look upon them. When such an occasion arose, Claver would throw his cloak over the person to hide the sight of broken flesh. Claver found many uses for his cloak as he served and soon his cloak became famous. Many who touched it were healed. Some even fought to claim even a piece of this powerful witness of God's healing power.

Peter Claver went from town to town, ministering to the needs of the slaves. His ministry reached legendary status. European settlers coveted his ministration, but Claver would never give special service to them. They had to wait, just as the African slaves waited to be served. Claver insisted that he first serve those he was committed to.[22]

# WILLIAM SEYMOUR—THE HUMBLE MAN OF GOD

Some of the attendees at the service jeered the unassuming and humble William Seymour as he stood before the crowd, calling out to God. Hundreds had gathered at the Azusa Street Mission, a former stable converted into a church. Many did not share the skeptical criticism of the few who sat in the back of the crowded sanctuary. Some shouted for joy, while others sat in their seats crying until the tears ran like rivers to the floor. More lay prostrate on the floor, calling out to God to cleanse them and fill them with the Holy Spirit.

The congregation witnessng this great outpouring of God's spiritual gifts was not one you would expect to see in the early twentieth century. The room was filled with people of many different nations and races, both male and female. The Holy Spirit's call brought them together for one purpose—to seek the Lord. William Seymour led the invitation and God showed himself strong.

William J. Seymour was born in 1870 to former slaves Simon and Phyllis Seymour. He spent most of his life working odd jobs, the best he could do as an illiterate. William found his calling at a church in Indiana called the Evening Light Saints, also known as the Church of God Reformation Movement. There he struggled with his calling. He contracted smallpox, which left him blind in his left eye. Soon after this sickness, he began to travel as an itinerant minister.

Seymour's ministry crossed racial borders and united people of all races under one purpose—an awakening to the Spirit of God. Numerous thousands were affected by the Azusa Street Mission, and it became a worldwide phenomenon. People from all over the globe came to see and experience the oftentimes radical manifestations of worship and prayer in the small stable-turned-church in California.

Charges of heresy and fanaticism were brought against the church, due to the radical and sometimes troublesome things that occurred in the mission. Yet Seymour believed that the people should worship God the way they felt was best, just as long as it was God they were worshiping.

Prompted by financial need and a desire to travel across the country to preach, Seymour left the church in the hands of two men—one by the name of William Durham. William Durham held meetings in the church while Seymour was out of town, and his preaching greatly restored the crowds that had attended in former years. But doctrinal differences often caused him to clash with Seymour. In their final confrontation, Durham left the Azusa Street Mission, and the crowds followed.

Seymour never was able to restore the huge attendance that once existed at his mission. He died at the age of 52, and after the amazing impact of his ministry, only 200 people attended his funeral. However, his ministry had reached the right people. Years after his death, it became clear that most Pentecostal churches could trace their roots directly to the events that occurred at the Azusa Street Mission. In fact, Bishop C. H. Mason, founder of the Church of God in Christ, was one of the many people touched by the ministry of William Seymour. The COGIC would not have been the same had not Bishop Mason traveled to the mission. He wrote of the power of God at the meetings, saying:

> *The sound of a mighty wind was in me and my soul cried, "Jesus, only, one like you." My soul cried and soon I began to die. It seemed that I heard the groaning of Christ on the cross dying for me. All of the work was in me until I died out of the old man. The sound stopped for a little while. My soul cried, "Oh, God, finish your work in me . . ."*

Through the power of the Holy Spirit at the Azusa Street Mission, God did indeed finish his work in C. H. Mason, just as He did for tens of thousands of other people through the humble man of God, William J. Seymour. The rebirth of Pentecost is often attributed to the events that occurred in the Azusa Street mission and continues today through many of the largest African-American denominations in the country.

# MARIA STEWART—SAYING WHAT NO ONE ELSE WOULD

Orphaned at only five years old in 1808, Maria was sent to work as a servant girl in a preacher's family. For ten years she served with no idea that the fire that existed inside her heart would be used for a purpose that would inspire black women to strive to become all that they could be.

Maria worked as a domestic servant long after her time with the preacher's family. She learned how to read in a Sabbath school and took classes in religious instruction. Her fight to learn to read would not be her final struggle with the forces that tried to hinder her progress in life.

In 1826, Maria had a short-lived marriage to James W. Stewart, a much older man, who died and left her widowed at only twenty-six years old. James Stewart, a wealthy man, planned to leave her an inheritance, but Maria was tricked into giving up the estate by a group of white businessmen.

With a passion to know Jesus Christ in an intimate way, Maria Stewart became an outspoken critic of the political and religious scene of her day. She rightfully believed that the culture, even among blacks, was sexist. She also believed that the black men of Boston's African-American community, the "sons of Africa," with little ambition, had "lost their souls."

Maria studied Daniel Walker's *Appeal to the Colored Citizens of the World* and began to write and speak as an independent, itinerant lecturer. The year was 1831. At that time, even in the North there was little opportunity for blacks, especially black women.

Maria suffered much opposition in order to continue to lecture—even opposition from black men. With this challenge, her faith and trust in God came forward in earnest.

Initially her public lectures were met with jeers and disapproval. Many accused her of speaking about religion too often in the public discourse. Much of this criticism had to do with the fact that she was a woman. Still, she continued to speak what she felt God had placed in her heart.

> *During the short period of my Christian warfare, I have indeed had to contend against the fiery darts of the devil. And was it not that the righteous are kept by the mighty power of God through faith unto salvation, long before this I should have proved to be like the seed by the way-side. For it has actually appeared to me at different periods, as though the powers of earth and hell had combined against me, to prove my overthrow. Yet amidst their dire attempts, I have found the Almighty to be "a friend that sticketh closer than a brother." He never will forsake the soul that leans on Him; though He chastens and corrects, it is for the soul's best interest. "And as a Father pitieth his children, so the Lord pitieth them that fear Him."*

> *But some of you have said, "do not talk so much about*

*religion, the people do not wish to hear you. We know
these things, tell us something we do not know." If you
know these things, my dear friends, and have performed
them, far happier, and more prosperous would you now
have been. "He that knoweth his Lord's will and obeyeth
it not, shall be beaten with many stripes." Sensible of
this, I have, regardless of the frowns and scoffs of a
guilty world, plead up religion, and the pure principles of
morality among you. Religion is the most glorious theme
that mortals can converse upon. The older it grows the
more new beauties it displays. Earth, with its brilliant
attractions, appears mean and sordid when compared to
it. It is that fountain that has no end, and those that
drink thereof shall never thirst; for it is, indeed, a well of
water springing up in the soul unto everlasting life.*[25]

Stewart became the nation's first black female political writer.
And while her writing had become controversial to both blacks and
whites, she spoke and wrote from her heart. The persecution
continued to the point that she had to leave Boston because she had
become the enemy of far too many people, both powerful and weak.
In her farewell address to the Bostonians, she wrote of the fact that
she was misinterpreted, by stating,

*For several years my heart was in continual sorrow. And
I believe that the Almighty beheld from His holy
habitation, the affliction wherewith I was afflicted, and
heard the false misrepresentations wherewith I was*

*misrepresented, and there was none to help. Then I cried unto the Lord in my troubles. And thus for wise and holy purposes, best known to himself, He has raised me in the midst of my enemies, to vindicate my wrongs before this people; and to reprove them for sin, as I have reasoned to them of righteousness and judgment to come. "For as the heavens are higher than the earth, so are His ways above our ways, and His thoughts above our thoughts." I believe, that for wise and holy purposes, best known to himself, He hath unloosed my tongue and put His word into my mouth, in order to confound and put all those to shame that have rose up against me. For He hath clothed my face with steel, and lined my forehead with brass. He hath put His testimony within me, and engraven His seal on my forehead. And with these weapons I have indeed set the fiends of earth and hell at defiance.*[24]

Stewart's life demonstrated an ability to go against the flow and still make a difference in this world. She eventually left Boston, and her time as a political activist, in the year 1833. From there, the fire in her heart continued to burn in New York, where her ministry became person-to-person, as a teacher. Later, she became a teacher in Baltimore, and then Washington. She was a champion for literacy among blacks and women.

## JEREMIAH ASHER—PROTESTING THE PEW

For the most part, northern blacks were free from the tyranny of slavery which spread across the South of the United States, yet opportunity did not knock at the door of every black male and female born in the northern part of the country. Doors slammed shut everywhere because of the inherent racism that permeated American culture. Jeremiah Asher faced a situation in the nineteenth century that shook the very foundations of the ungodly system that existed behind church doors.

One Sunday morning Jeremiah entered the large sanctuary at First Baptist Church where he was a member. On this occasion, he arrived very late and found nowhere to sit and worship. Scanning the sanctuary, he finally looked over to where he normally sat and realized that his seat was taken. His was no ordinary seat. It was a special pew which he described as, "six-feet square, with the sides so high it was almost impossible to see the minister or the rest of the congregation." It was made to accommodate about fifteen to twenty people. This was considered the "Negro pew."

Jeremiah did not take his normal seat that morning. However, he also did not take one of the general seats in the congregation, reserved only for whites. He quietly went and sat in another seat that was open in the "Negro pews" and listened to the sermon that morning. On leaving the church that day, he resolved that he would never set foot in that church again. He was as good as his word and never went in again.

Other church members noticed his sudden absence and eventually questioned him about his reasons. He was hesitant to give an answer at first, but then told them plainly once he was pressed to explain himself. He was determined to stand by his resolution not to ever set foot in that church again.

By then, the leaders of the church were confounded. With the societal prejudice of the time, few could understand the reason for his dissatisfaction. Why would a man be so angry about something so simple as a church pew? But to Asher this dispute was about much more than a church pew—it was about equality and common sense.

> I contended that those seats which were made for whites were good enough for blacks; if they did not wish to mix us together, they could give us a certain number of seats expressly for colored persons. But they [church leaders] were aware that, without some visible distinction, whites coming in would often be sitting in the Negro seats, and their devotions would be frequently disturbed by the pew-opener, who would be obliged to remove them, and regulate all such irregularities. . . . If men will disenfranchise and separate me from the rest of my Father's children, they shall do it at their own expense, not mine. I cannot prevent it, but I will not help them do it. I will lift up my voice against it.[25]

Eventually, better pews were constructed for the black

members. But for Jeremiah Asher, the issue was not the appearance of the pew but the separation of God's children. Interestingly, these special pews did not allow free access to the house of God. They had to be rented at the cost of a dollar per year. As expected, few people used the new, improved rental pews.

Later, Asher was invited to a meeting to settle this issue once and for all. The pastor of the church, J. S. Eaton, began inquiring of each black member as to their objections to the new, beautiful rental pews that had been made for them. He questioned all of the other members before questioning Asher. None of them voiced any objections. This may seem surprising, but in that day, relatively few people spoke out about such injustices, as they were looked upon as the norm and were accepted. But Asher was not one to conform to an unjust system—especially not in a church.

> *Then, they inquired what I had to say; when I rose up from my seat and addressed them for about twenty or thirty minutes, and if ever I felt the presence of God, it was that day. I was not replied to by the chair or any one of the assembly. It was agreed to report to the church favorably. The committee members were satisfied; the coloured members might sit where they pleased in the galleries, and that was the end of this revolution.*[26]

God revealed to Jeremiah Asher the reason He had called this reluctant crusader to confront an ungodly system. Asher accepted a call to preach the gospel soon after this incident. He later withdrew once again from First Baptist Church and organized a ministry in Providence, Rhode Island, then went on to serve as a pastor in Philadelphia.

God uses foolish things to confound the wise. Jeremiah Asher confronted a seemingly foolish situation to bring out far deeper issues that existed around him.

# JERMAIN W. LOUGEN—VALIANT RESCUER

In 1851 the Liberty party convention was just getting started, created by Abolitionists who believed in taking political action to further anti-slavery goals. While the convention was in full swing, something tragic happened in the same town of Syracuse, New York. William Henry, a fugitive slave, was recaptured by a United States Marshall. He was placed in shackles, imprisoned, and detailed to be transported back to the South.

Church bells rang at the crowded convention to gather attention to this troubling news, and a large number of brave Americans of mixed races came together to prevent the Fugitive Slave Act of 1850 from being enforced. The Fugitive Slave Act made it possible for the government to arrest and detain any fugitive slave, and to punish all who prevented slaves in any way from being arrested.[27]

In the hearts and minds of those attending the Liberty party convention, this act was the final straw. The leaders of the Liberty party decided to prevent its enforcement, even to their own peril. Members of the party stormed the office and jail where the fugitive slave was held, rescued him, and transported him to Canada, where he would be assured asylum.

Jermain W. Loguen was one of those valiant rescuers who took part in saving the life of the fugitive, William Henry. Loguen had himself been a slave who escaped to Canada in 1834. After receiving an education in numerous institutions in the North, he became a preacher and settled in Syracuse, New York.

Due in large part to his appeal to the Liberty party, officials decided to make Syracuse an open city for all fugitive slaves to seek safety within its borders.

*Now, you are assembled here, the strength of this city is here to express their sense of this fugitive act, and to proclaim to the despots at Washington whether it shall be enforced here—whether you will permit the government to return me and other fugitives who have sought an asylum among you, to the Hell of slavery. The question is with you. If you will give us up, say so, and we will shake the dust from our feet and leave you. But we believe better things. We know you are taken by surprise. The immensity of this meeting testifies to the general consternation that has brought it together, necessarily, precipitately, to decide the most stirring question that can be presented, to wit, whether, the government having transgressed constitutional and natural limits, you will bravely resist its aggressions, and tell its soulless agents that no slave-holder shall make your city and county a hunting field for slaves.*

*Whatever may be your decision, my ground is taken. I have declared it everywhere. It is known over the State and out of the state— over the line in the North, and over the line in the South. I don't respect this law—I don't fear it—I won't obey it! It outlaws me, and I outlaw it, and the men who attempt to enforce it on me.*

*I place the governmental officials on the ground that
they place me. I will not live a slave, and if force is
employed to re-enslave me, I shall make preparations to
meet the crisis as becomes a man. If you will stand by
me—and I believe you will do it, for your freedom and
honor are involved as well as mine—it requires no
microscope to see that—I say if you will stand with us in
resistance to this measure, you will be the saviours of
your country. Your decision to-night in favor of resistance
will give vent to the spirit of liberty, and it will break the
bands of party, and shout for joy all over the North.
Your example only is needed to be the type of popular
action in Auburn, and Rochester, and Utica, and
Buffalo, and all the West, and eventually in the Atlantic
cities. Heaven knows that this act of noble daring will
break out somewhere—may God grant that Syracuse be
the honored spot, whence it shall send an earthquake
voice through the land![28]*

The words of Jermain Loguen sent an earthquake among those
who heard this impassioned speech, and the Liberty party, as well
as the entire Abolitionist movement, continued on in full force.

Jerry Loguen died in 1872, having served as a minister and
activist. His moment in history was fulfilled. A single speech helped
create a safe city that defied the law, yet embraced the idea of
creating a refuge for fugitive slaves.

## DANIEL ALEXANDER PAYNE—BISHOP AND ACTIVIST

*Born in a slave-holding State, with little or no advantages of education—indeed, with almost insuperable obstacles placed in his way—he yet succeeded in making himself proficient in many branches of learning, and so qualified himself as to be able to instruct others. How eloquently does this life, out of the difficulties with which it had to contend, and the grand results which were the outcome of his earnest, self-sacrificing labors, plead with the young men and women of to-day to seize the flying moments, freighted as they are with priceless opportunities for improvement! It shows the value of a high purpose steadily adhered to. In infancy he was consecrated by a godly father and mother to the service of God. With this idea he began life, and along that line he has steadily marched during all these years; and from the summit of this high resolve he will one day step out of this world to be forever with God.*

*It shows how, with proper care and attention, the smallest gifts may be made to yield a large return. Naturally of a weak constitution, he has, by husbanding his strength, been enabled to do an amount of work which is perfectly astonishing; and to-day, although far advanced in years, he is still actively engaged in the arduous duties of his position. It shows the importance of order if any thing is to be accomplished. His life has been a thoroughly systematic one. A time for every thing and every thing in its time has been with him a ruling principle of action during all his life, and will account for the large amount of work which he has been enabled to accomplish. For many years he has risen at five o'clock in the morning, winter and summer; has had the same time for study whether at home or away. And this system or order has been carried into every part of his busy life, and with the happiest effect, both upon his personal character and in the results which have flowed from his labors.*

*His life has also its lesson of humility, blended with a high sense of official responsibility. One of the most striking chapters in the book is that which describes his election to the bishopric. When first approached on the subject he positively refused to allow his name to be used. And when, four years later, he was literally forced into it, the effect of his election upon him reveals to us a spirit as rare as it is beautiful. To quote his own words: "I trembled from head to foot, and wept. I knew that I was unworthy of the office, because I had neither the physical strength, the learning, nor the sanctity which make one fit for such a high, holy, and responsible position." These words ought to be written in letters of gold, and carefully commended to all aspirants after ecclesiastical honors. How great the contrast between the noble spirit which they exhibit and the unworthy greed for power and position which characterizes, alas! too many in the Church to-day!*[29]

Daniel Payne waited anxiously to meet the President of the United States, in order to hear what his heart longed to know—that the slaves of the District of Columbia would be freed. Congress had already passed the bill, and it was now up to the President to sign it into law.

Daniel Payne was the Bishop of the African Methodist Episcopal Church. He had been highly active in the rights of blacks all of his life, and his journey took him all the way to the seats of power in the United States.

Born of free parents in South Carolina, Daniel became an orphan at the age of nine and a half. At thirteen, he began learning the carpenter's trade, where he spent most of his teenage years. In his late teens he came into contact with something that would change his life—a self-interpreting Bible. He learned how to read, first from his adopted father, and then from his subsequent schooling. The Bible's content excited his intellect, as well as his spiritual needs.

The man who compiled this Bible never received any formal schooling in the languages of Hebrew, Greek, or Latin. Daniel felt that if the Bible expositor, John Brown, could accomplish such a great thing, why couldn't he accomplish something equally as great?

So there he sat, waiting for an answer from the President.

*He answered and said: "There was a company of gentlemen here to-day requesting me by no means to sign it." To which Senator Schurz replied: "But, Mr. President, there will be a committee to beg that you fail not to sign it; for all Europe is looking to see that you fail not." Then said I: "Mr. President, you will remember that on the eve of your departure from Springfield, Ill., you begged the citizens of the republic to pray for you." He said, "Yes." Said I: "From that moment we, the colored citizens of the republic, have been praying: 'O Lord, just as Thou didst cause the throne of David to wax stronger and stronger, while that of Saul should wax weaker and weaker, so we beseech Thee cause the power at Washington to grow stronger and stronger, while that at Richmond shall grow weaker and weaker.'" Slightly bending his head, the President said: "Well, I must believe that God has led me thus far, for I am conscious that I never would have accomplished what has been done if He had not been with me to counsel and to shield." But neither Carl Schurz nor I could induce him to say "Yes" or "No" to our direct question.*[30]

Slavery ended in the District of Columbia on April 16, 1862. Lincoln's answer was clearly "yes." Daniel Alexander Payne's desire was fulfilled.

He was the official historian of the AME Church, an educator, and a highly influential bishop. It is arguable which accomplishment of his was the greatest. However, this one thing rings true: it all started with a Bible. It was in the pages of this great book that Daniel Alexander Payne saw his own greatness, as well as his need for a Savior.

## ISAAC LANE—FROM SLAVE TO SCHOLAR

In 1834, a man was born who would give his life to the encouragement and inspiration of his fellow slaves. He was reared almost motherless and fatherless, without parental care or guidance. For this reason, God became his Father. At an early age, he had a conception of God, but it was not until he was twenty-one that he actually confessed his faith in Jesus Christ. Soon after his confession of faith, he accepted a calling from God to preach.

*After the Civil War I established regular hours for the studying and the reading of God's Word, and these I have kept all of these years. I coveted the morning hours the most, although in the evening, when the hours for work were over, I would read and meditate until my candlelight or pine torch would fail me or my body would succumb to fatigue and I would fall asleep. The Bible, Binney's "Theological Compend," Clarke's "Commentaries," Watson's "Bible Dictionary," and Ralston's "Elements of Divinity" were among the first books that I studied. These books I read with a fascination from which I have not escaped to this day.[31]*

Strangely he strove to put an end to this calling by ignoring it. He was not successful. Through wise counsel and encouragement, he firmly decided to enter the work of the ministry. Yet, when he applied for a license to preach, the response he got was not an encouraging one. He was told that the Methodist Episcopal Church did not believe in granting licenses to blacks. This information did not change his resolve, but rather, drew him to prayer. Years later, the church changed its course and overturned their divisive views on ordination. Isaac Lane's course stayed the same, and he was granted a license to preach, but not without proof of his merit as a learned Bible scholar.

Isaac Lane, the former slave, was questioned on nearly every phrase concerning the doctrine of Christ. He passed with flying colors. But major challenges were to come, as the Civil War had just ended and the South was doomed to defeat.

*The Emancipation Proclamation that had been prepared by President Abraham Lincoln in the month of July, of the year 1862, was not issued until January 1 of the year 1863. It did not go into effect at this time, as we all know, but its influence was felt at once the country over. A studious effort was made on the part of a good many people to keep the issuance of this proclamation a profound secret to the Negroes. But it could not be done. There was too much excitement for such a clever piece of work to be done with any degree of success, and there were too many Negroes who were able to read and understand the trend of affairs to be misled by any subterfuge that might be resorted to by the sympathizers of the Lost Cause. The Confederacy was doomed, and this proclamation was the death knell to slavery on the American continent. The moral effect was wonderful.*

*Strong men who had put all their faith in the supremacy of the Confederate army now began to weaken and became despaired of success. The slaves saw it, and it required great effort on their part to suppress their feelings of rejoicing.*

*After Lee had surrendered and the Confederacy had gone to pieces and Jefferson Davis had become a refugee, our owners called us together and told us we were free and had to take care of ourselves. There I was with a large, dependent family to support. I had no money, no education, no mother nor father to whom to look for help in any form.*

*Our former owners prophesied that half of us would starve, but not so. It must be admitted, however, that we had a hard time, and it seemed at times that the prophecy would come true; but the harder the time, the harder we worked and the more we endured. For six months we lived on nothing but bread, milk, and water. We had a time to keep alive; but by praying all the time, with faith in God, and believing that He would provide for His own, we saved enough to get the next year not only bread, milk, and water, but meat also.*[34]

God was faithful to the Lane family, even in the most trying of circumstances. He became to Isaac that "stream in the desert," or that "lily in the valley." Soon after this time, Isaac was able to devote his time to the ministry, and founded an organization called the Colored Methodist Episcopal Church in America.

Through many overwhelming trials, including the death of Isaac's son and the loss of much personal property to fire, this new ministry eventually spanned the nation, holding many conferences year after year. Isaac Lane also founded Lane College in Jackson, Tennessee, which thrives to this day.

Temporary setbacks, poverty, and even the despair of life could not stop Isaac Lane from being all that he was destined to be. He did not fall to a prophecy of defeat. The words of those who enslaved him were meant to cause a severe bruise to his confidence. And perhaps there were days when his confidence was greatly diminished. But even then, Isaac Lane held in his heart a vision that would bring education and scholarship to many thousands.

# AMANDA SMITH—THE SINGING PILGRIM

The hot sun glared down upon the missionary group in Calcutta, India. One preacher after another had come to share the gospel, and many of them were roughly handled by the locals in the area. Now, the missionary J. M. Thoburn was scheduled to speak to the crowd. A large group of young men and boys gathered together, expecting Mr. Thoburn to meet the same fate as his predecessors. These men and boys were successful at breaking up the crowd who were intent on listening to the gospel message. Their cries and gestures toward Thoburn were clear—he would receive a beating.

All would have been lost, but there was an unlikely secret weapon—a weapon of prayer in the person of a small African-American woman who traveled with the missionary—Amanda Smith.

Amanda stood before the crowd in the midst of all the mayhem, kneeled on the ground with her face towards Heaven, and poured out her soul in prayer. The increasingly rowdy crowd was transfixed on the spot. Not even a whisper interrupted the prayer of this woman of God. An unseen power flowed through her which demanded silence from everyone.

Once Amanda finished praying, the crowd calmed, the men and boys stopped their marauding, and the service went on in an orderly fashion. The prayer of Amanda Smith could very well have saved numerous lives. More importantly, her prayers were instrumental in the saving of numerous souls. Later, Thoburn wrote the following of her:

> *Her remarks on the Bible lesson did not particularly impress me, and it was not until the evening of the same day, when I chanced to be kneeling near her at a prayer meeting, that I became impressed that she was a person of more than ordinary power.*
>
> *The meetings of the day had not been very successful, and a spirit of depression rested upon many of the leaders. A heavy rain had fallen, and we were kneeling somewhat uncomfortably in the straw which surrounded the preacher's stand.*
>
> *A number had prayed, and I was myself sharing the general feeling of depression, when I was suddenly startled by the voice of song. I lifted my head, and at a short distance, probably not more than two yards from me, I saw the colored sister of the morning kneeling in an upright position, with her hands spread out and her face all aglow.*
>
> *She had suddenly broken out with a triumphant song, and while I was startled by the change in the order of the meeting, I was at once absorbed with interest in the song and the singer.*
>
> *Something like a hallowed glow seemed to rest upon the dark face before me, and I felt in a second that she was possessed of a rare degree of spiritual power.*

*That invisible something which we are accustomed to call power, and which is never possessed by any Christian believer except as one of the fruits of the indwelling Spirit of God, was hers in a marked degree.*

*From that time onward I regarded her as a gifted worker in the Lord's vineyard, but I had still to learn that the enduement of the Spirit had given her more than the one gift of spiritual power.*

*A week later I met her at Lakeside, Ohio, and was again impressed in the same way, but I then began to discover that she was not only a woman of faith, but that she possessed a clearness of vision which I have seldom found equaled.*

*Her homely illustrations, her quaint expressions, her warmhearted appeals, all possess the supreme merit of being so many vehicles for conveying the living truths of the Gospel of Jesus Christ to the hearts of those who are fortunate enough to hear her.*[33]

The missionary team traveled through Western Europe, all the way through Africa and India, winning souls to Christ and successfully praying for the healing of many. While Amanda Smith's accomplishments were great, they sprung from humble beginnings.

Amanda, unlike most of her colleagues, was born a slave. Without formal training in ministry, she used all she had to minister to the native Indians. All she had was the love of God.

Even with all of her missionary experience and accomplishments, she returned to the United States only to face opposition to her preaching by those of her own race. She was a woman, and many took great care in trying to keep her "in her place." But in Amanda's mind, her "place" was in service to God, and she determined to please God rather than obey the fabricated cultural limitations that were placed upon her by those who surrounded her.

She had ministered in Asia, established schools in Africa, and preached the gospel throughout Europe. Many of her African-American contemporaries had not accomplished half of what she had already done in her life. Yet, the discrimination continued.

In 1871, the African Methodist Episcopal Church held their annual conference in Nashville, Tennessee. Amanda Smith had an opportunity to go to the conference.

> *I ventured to ask one of the brethren, who had been elected delegate, to tell me how much it would cost to go to Nashville; I would like to go if it did not cost too much.*
>
> *He looked at me in surprise, mingled with half disgust; the very idea of one looking like me to want to go to General Conference; they cut their eye at my big poke, Quaker bonnet, with not a flower, not a feather. He said, "I tell you, Sister, it will cost money to go down there; and if you ain't got plenty of it, it's no use to go;" and*

*turned away and smiled; another said:*

*"What does she want to go for?"*

*"Woman preacher; they want to be ordained," was the reply.*

*"I mean to fight that thing," said the other. "Yes, indeed, so will I," said another.*

*Then a slight look to see if I took it in. I did; but in spite of it all I believed God would have me go. He knew that the thought of ordination had never once entered my mind, for I had received my ordination from Him, Who said, "Ye have not chosen Me, but I have chosen you, and ordained you, that you might go and bring forth fruit, and that your fruit might remain."*[34]

Amanda Smith not only attended the general conference, but she also, by God's favor, sang at the conference. She was spotted by someone who had known her earlier in her ministry. Amanda Smith stood at the podium and sang, and as she describes it, the Spirit of God seemed to fall on all the people.

*The preachers got happy. They wept and shouted "Amen!" "Praise the Lord!" At the close a number of them came to me and shook hands, and said, "God bless you, sister. Where did you come from? I would like to have you come on my charge." Another would say, "Look here, sister, when are you going home? God bless you. I would like to have you come to my place." And so it went. So that after that many of my brethren believed in me, especially as the question of ordination of women never was mooted in the Conference.*

*But how they have advanced since then. Most of them believe in the ordination of women, and I believe some have been ordained. But I am satisfied with the ordination that the Lord has given me. Praise His name!*

*Even with my own people, in this country, I have not always met with the pleasantest things. But still I have not backslidden, nor felt led to leave the church. His grace has ever been sufficient. And all we need to-day is to trust Him.*

> *"Simply trusting every day,*
> *Trusting through the stormy way,*
> *Even when my faith is small,*
> *Trusting Jesus, that is all."*[35]

Amanda Smith continued in the ministry of the gospel until she went home to be with her Savior in 1915. Never to be denied the service of her God, she stood firm when others told her to kneel to the oppressive and hurtful discrimination of her day. Many who did not believe in women preaching the gospel did not take into account Amanda Smith, the singing pilgrim. She was one in whom God believed.

# ROSA YOUNG—EDUCATING WITH GOD'S HELP

It is very easy to look into a classroom of students and not realize the sacrifice involved in bringing an education to every child. Easy, unless the year is 1912, and all the children, faculty, and teachers are African Americans.

A woman named Rosa Young stood in the front of the classroom—the founder of the Rosebud School. She was able to educate a generation of rural children with hard work and faith in God, empowering them to be more than they could ever have been without her work.

*It was not the thought of money that induced me to be willing to assume the heavy burden, the weighty responsibility, and the binding obligation to buy land, erect a building, and operate a school for the benefit of my race. There was no money appropriated or set aside in any form for the support of such a difficult task or great and expensive undertaking. There was no outside source to draw on, no board, no organization, no philanthropist backing it, not even the promise of as much as one penny from a single individual. The whole situation depended on me. To start with, I was to be the board, the bank, and the organization.*

*Now, what did I have? Nothing. I was no wealthy woman possessing great riches, owning a number of investments producing large incomes. I had the pitiful*

*sum of two-hundred dollars, my own personal money, the
sum I had saved above my personal use besides what I
had to give my parents to help them along with the
support of my younger brothers and sisters. What was
the meager sum, all my little living, against such an
expensive undertaking? And yet I was willing to give it,
and give it gladly, for the benefit and uplift of my
destitute race, and for the spreading of Christ's
kingdom.[36]*

These words flowed from the heart of a woman who had set
out to start a school and establish a learning institution for the poor,
destitute blacks in her rural hometown. She could have found
opportunity elsewhere, but desired no position of power, although
she was college educated and highly intelligent. Her greatest
concern was for the "least of these."

Observing the pathetic condition of her brothers and sisters,
the ignorance, the superstition, and the lack of morals that
permeated her community, she felt it necessary to educate the
rejected and downtrodden.

*I always believed in education of the heart; for a bright
head with a wicked heart stands for naught. It only
tends to breed trouble. I knew something was wrong with
the kind of religion my people had, but I did not know
what was wrong about it. I desired a better Christian
training for myself and my people, but I did not know
where to find it.*

*The Lord our Savior who loved us saw all of this and had compassion on us. He saw that the sad plight of our immortal souls was far worse than our physical condition. The Lord looked down from heaven upon us. He saw this hellward-leading teaching, this man-made doctrine of salvation by works. He saw darkness had covered our land. Our eyes were blind to the knowledge contained in His blessed Gospel. The Lord saw that we were all on the wrong road, regardless of how well we meant, and could never reach heaven that way.*

*God saw that I was concerned, that I was worried, about the many things pertaining to the temporal welfare of my people. God saw my eager desires and longings to do something for Him and my race. I did not have the least idea of what was to be done. I could not preach, for women are not allowed to preach. But the Lord instilled in me the thought of building a school, gave me strength to begin this work, and sustained me.*[37]

Rosa was a prophet who cried out from her heart the truth the desperate need for her people. She felt strongly that a post-slavery darkness had covered her people and that she was called to shine a light. The Rosebud School in Rosebud, Alabama was completed in 1912, and opened with only seven children in a small shed.

Rosa was concerned for the souls of her people. She was able to work around the discrimination of her day by influencing lives with what God had blessed her with—an education. Her highest ambition was to serve God and her people. She gave religious instruction, academic teaching, and leadership to the poorest of the poor in her community. In only three years, the attendance of the Rosebud School grew from 7 to 215 children—quite an astounding feat for a school in a rural, sparsely populated area.

# S. Mattie Fisher and Jessie Mapp— Building a Center for God

*We need a trained ministry to teach our people. They need more teaching than preaching. They need to be taught the Word of God and not an appeal made to the emotional side of their lives.*

--Jessie Mapp

*We are making a general survey of the district to find our people with the idea of establishing a community center for them at the church at Thirty-first Street and South Park Avenue. In this connection, we are making a house to house visit to all the people from 28th street to 39th street, and from State Street to the Lake. We are asking the names of all the grown people of the home, their church connection, if any, how long they have been in the city, their experience as Christian workers in their home churches, their occupation and the number, ages and sex of their children. Will you please give this information?*

Repeatedly Miss Fisher recited this short speech from door to door. Many who heard it did not even understand what she was saying, and had to have it spelled out for them word for word until they finally understood. To save time, Miss Fisher and her fellow surveyor, Jessie Mapp, split up to cover different parts of town. In the end, they made 5,082 visits. This survey became the basis of all the activities that went on in the Olivet Christian Center in Chicago.

Fisher was one of the first trained black social workers in the United States. In 1918 she and Jessie Mapp went door-to-door to find out how they could best assist the new migrants from the South—the former slaves and descendants of slaves who had traveled North to find opportunity.

Aside from the survey, they made nearly 700 visits to the sick, disheartened, and shut-ins. They moved from house to house, presenting themselves as living examples of God's love towards those in need of a friend, a servant, or a healer.

Within eight months, the Olivet Christian Center began in earnest and was a place for Christian development. The two women taught young married women, adult class meetings, and other social gatherings. Their work resulted in many conversions and new members of the Olivet First Baptist Church. Mattie Fisher's greatest joy was in knowing that she played a part in bringing someone into the saving knowledge of Jesus Christ.

Very often Christian work seems to be menial. Yet, S. Mattie Fisher took a menial job and turned it into something great. By the 1930s, Olivet First Baptist Church grew to over twelve thousand members and became the largest church in the entire nation. But it could not have grown without the tenacity of one woman and her committed partner in vision. Their diligence took the church to a place it could never have gone without their godly and humble service.[38]

## NANNIE H. BURROUGHS—SPECIALIZING IN THE WHOLLY IMPOSSIBLE

*Note this fact about our religious life: "Five out of every eleven Negroes in the United States are church members." This should mean a high spiritual and religious life, but it does not. We are wont to substitute shouting for service.*

--NANNIE HELEN BURROUGHS

*The Master's voice is clearer today than it was Two-Thousand years ago, when, in the midst of the Judean and Galilean sin and perdition and wickedness in high places, He turned from the woman at the well and rebukingly said to His disciples who marveled that He had talked with her, "Lift up your eyes and look on the fields, for they are white already to harvest."*

*He speaks to the twenty-five million Protestants in America and says to them, "Look at the condition of the fifty-eight million unchurched Protestants in your own land, and apply my religious and social program to their needs, sufferings and appeals. Build up the waste places of the nations."*[39]

Nannie Helen Burroughs was a straight talker in the strongest sense of the word. But she was far more than talk. She studied business and domestic science in high school, a high level of education in the late 1800s, and went on to obtain an honorary masters degree which completed her academic education.

Her heart was to offer Christian women the highest development of Christian womanhood, with a goal to start a school that would emphasize practical and professional skills. She believed that authentic Christianity was the key to racial regeneration. While a committed member of the church, she was often a staunch critic of how it was run. One major concern she had was that the majority of the church consisted of women, but the decision-making power was exclusive to men—men who, in her opinion, were often unwise in their business practices and unable to effectively run with the vision of the ministry in those changing times. She was more than just a critic. Her criticism came with clear-cut plans for the future stemming from her business training.

Nannie Burroughs died in 1961, at the age of 81. She did not meet the day of her death before starting a school for women, which trained black women to become financially independent. She also managed to acquire commercial property during the Great Depression. She proved that there was nothing impossible for the person who believed in and trusted God.

# FREDERICK DOUGLASS—GREATNESS IN CHAINS

> *What was possible for me is possible for you. Do not*
> *think because you are colored you cannot accomplish*
> *anything. Strive earnestly to add to your knowledge. So*
> *long as you remain in ignorance, so long will you fail to*
> *command the respect of your fellow men.*
>
> --FREDERICK DOUGLASS

Even at the young age of thirteen, young Frederick longed for a relationship with someone he could call "Father" and "Protector." He often spent great amounts of time in loneliness and destitution, calling upon someone, somewhere, to rescue him from the void that filled his soul. When he was older, that void was filled with the love and mercy of God.

> *I cannot say that I had a very distinct notion of what*
> *was required of me, but one thing I did know well: I was*
> *wretched and had no means of making myself otherwise.*

> *I consulted a good colored man named Charles Lawson,*
> *and in tones of holy affection he told me to pray, and to*
> *"cast all my care upon God." This I sought to do; and*
> *though for weeks I was a poor, broken-hearted mourner,*
> *traveling through doubts and fears, I finally found my*
> *burden lightened and my heart relieved. I loved all*
> *mankind, slaveholders not excepted, though I abhorred*
> *slavery more than ever. I saw the world in a new light,*
> *and my great concern was to have everybody converted.*

> *My desire to learn increased, and especially, did I want a*
> *thorough acquaintance with the contents of the Bible. I*
> *have gathered scattered pages of the Bible from the filthy*
> *street-gutters, and washed and dried them, that in*
> *moments of leisure I might get a word or two of wisdom*
> *from them.*[40]

This event changed Frederick Douglass more than any other. He hungered for the Word of God as if his very life and destiny depended on its printed pages. In time he came to learn that it did.

His steadfast faith propelled him to accomplish more than most American citizens of his day and to become perhaps the greatest abolitionist that ever lived.

Frederick Douglass ran a secret Sunday school until his owner, Thomas Auld, found out about it and sent him to a "Negro-breaker." Frederick was whipped severely for the most menial reasons. One day Frederick fought back. He did not fight to kill his abuser, but only to stop him from going too far. He succeeded, and his abuser never laid a hand on him again. In the struggle with the "Negro-breaker," he realized that his abuser was a man—nothing more, nothing less. This knowledge and understanding brought the desire for liberty to the very core of his heart.

He eventually escaped slavery and headed north. In Rochester, New York, his name became synonymous with the abolitionist movement. Frederick Douglass united with the newly formed Republican Party in support of the candidacy of Abraham Lincoln.

Abe Lincoln was elected that year and soon after the Civil War began.

Douglass desperately wanted blacks to fight alongside Union soldiers for this cause. While the main purpose of the Civil War was, and continues to be, debatable, the purpose of the war as far as black Americans are concerned was clear—to end slavery in the South. The Union fought in the Civil War without blacks, initially. After suffering severe losses, it was clear that more troops were needed. When African-American troops hit the lines of battle, the tables turned in the Union's favor. The bloodiest war in American history ensued.

Because of Douglas' dedication to the abolitionist cause, millions of blacks walked away from the plantations that held them captive. Chains from every southern state that held slaves fell to the ground, and a cry of victory was heard in every slave home when it was learned that slavery had been defeated.

Frederick Douglass played a major part in this great victory. He eventually became a personal adviser to President Lincoln and the United States ambassador to Haiti.

A slave can shake the world when God is in him or her. Douglass had a charge to keep and a deep commitment to God. God came through, and Frederick Douglass will forever be one of the greatest Americans who ever lived.

## GEORGE WASHINGTON CARVER—CREATOR OF A NEW SCIENCE

*He was born in a crudely constructed log cabin on the farm of one Moses Carver, (a German) near Diamond Grove, Missouri, during the dark days of emancipation in 1864. Out of poverty and obscurity this little boy was destined to become an outstanding representative of his race; an apostle of good will between the races; a creative genius, and one of the greatest scientists the world has ever known.*

--RALPH M. MERRIT, CONCERNING GEORGE WASHINGTON CARVER

*This little boy got his name in a very unusual way. He was not so fortunate as to inherit a name, but because of his faithful devotion to his work, and also his habitual truthfulness about everything, the Carvers called him George Washington. He got the name Carver from the Carver family. He speaks of Mr. Carver as being a very humane man.*

*George began to seek knowledge at an early age. During the day he spent almost all of his time roving the woods, and acquainting himself with every flower and every peculiar weed. He was also interested in studying the rocks, and different stones, and the birds. He usually played by himself as his playmates were very few.*[41]

George Washington Carver grew up with a peculiar curiosity—he was obsessed with plant life. He worked to educate himself, despite the racial barriers of his day. These barriers did not stop him from getting a college education and becoming one of America's foremost scientists.

He graduated from Simpson College and later began to teach at the famed Tuskegee Institute, which was founded by Booker T. Washington. It was here that his work became famous all over the nation.

He taught local farmers how to make their lives easier, and earn more money, by using the simple but scientific techniques he presented before them. His work became known the world over. Stunningly, his most popular achievement was his innovation with the simple peanut. With it, he was able to teach others how to feed entire families and formulated recipes utilizing this simple legume. He came up with over three hundred uses for the peanut, and since there were massive amounts of peanuts produced, his ideas stimulated the economy of the time.

George Washington Carver had created a new science; he learned to make many different products out of ordinary plants. He transformed the agricultural industry of the day, and farmers from all over the nation are indebted to his genius.

# ELIJAH McCOY—CHANGING THE RAILWAY INDUSTRY

He was, indeed, the real McCoy. In fact, the phrase "the real McCoy," was coined because of the success of Elijah McCoy. Gifted as a child in handling tools and machines, Elijah was sent to a school in Scotland by his parents to study mechanical engineering. He learned how to design his inventions and create useful tools and simple machines. As a young man, he returned to the United States.

Despite his education and skills, no one would hire a black person for the type of job he was seeking. Elijah desired a job that would suit his skill. The only job he could get was as an oilman for the Central Railroad in Michigan. While accepting such a position seemed like the cursed destiny of far too many blacks during the 1800s, it actually proved to be the greatest blessing of Elijah McCoy's life. His job was to ensure that the train was lubricated. Through his ingenuity, he was able to be great at a job that many would consider menial.

The world may not know the head engineers of the trains Elijah McCoy worked on. They may not even know the head mechanics or the wealthiest passengers. But one thing is certain. The simple oilman and coal-thrower on the train—the black, lowest-ranked employee of the train—would become one of the most famous names of his day.

Elijah sought a way to alleviate the need to constantly stop the entire train just to lubricate it before continuing the voyage. This delay may not seem like a major issue, but it took over a mile to stop these trains, then long periods of time were spent working and getting the train running again.

In response to this problem, Elijah invented an oil cup that lubricated wherever it was needed—amazingly, while the train was moving. This invention transformed the freight industry, and people from all over the country sought Elijah's lubricating machine.

Elijah later invented items such as the ironing board and the lawn sprinkler. But whenever anyone wanted a lubricating machine for a train, they asked for the "real McCoy."

Greatness can be attained, even if the job at hand is not glorious. Elijah McCoy figured out how to be the best at what he was given to do.

# PHYLLIS WHEATLEY—CHRISTIAN POETESS AND SLAVE

Captured in Africa, the young child journeyed across the Atlantic in a slave vessel, which offered little comfort other than the knowledge that life still existed. The year was 1761, and Phyllis was now a slave.

*We cannot know at how early a period she was beguiled from the hut of her mother; or how long a time elapsed between her abduction from her first home and her being transferred to the abode of her benevolent mistress, where she must have felt like one awaking from a fearful dream. This interval was, no doubt, a long one; and filled, as it must have been, with various degrees and kinds of suffering, might naturally enough obliterate the recollection of earlier and happier days. The solitary exception which held its place so tenaciously in her mind, was probably renewed from day to day through this long season of affliction; for, every morning, when the bereaved child saw the sun emerging from the wide waters, she must have thought of her mother, prostrating herself before the first golden beam that glanced across her native plains.*

John Wheatley of Boston purchased Phyllis. Considering the cruelty of the day, he would have been the lesser of evils for this frail, humble seven-year-old child. The transaction completed,

Phyllis became his possession.

She was taken to the Wheatley home, put in more comfortable clothing, and given food. Upon observance, it seemed as though the young girl had uncommon intelligence for a seven-year-old. She began to make attempts to write, even then.

> *A daughter of Mrs. Wheatley, not long after the child's first introduction to the family, undertook to learn her to read and write; and, while she astonished her instructress by her rapid progress, she won the good will of her kind mistress, by her amiable disposition and the propriety of her behaviour. She was not devoted to menial occupations, as was at first intended; nor was she allowed to associate with the other domestics of the family, who were of her own color and condition, but was kept constantly about the person of her mistress.*[42]

As Phyllis grew older, her development as a writer increased greatly. Many books were given to her so that she could continue to study and increase in her ability to write. Soon, she would endeavor to master the Latin language.

Phyllis Wheatley became renowned for her unusual intellect, as it surpassed many of those whites who had been formally educated. Frequent visits by clergymen and high-society-types brought much attention to Wheatley, but her humble demeanor remained, until she began to write. It was in her writing that the fire inside her heart would burn with a passion upon the printed page.

*Ye martial powers, and all ye tuneful Nine,*
*Inspire my song, and aid my high design.*
*The dreadful scenes and toils of war I write,*
*The ardent warriors and the fields of fight:*
*You best remember, and you best can sing*
*The acts of heroes to the vocal string:*
*Resume the lays with which your sacred lyre,*
*Did then the poet and the sage inspire.*[45]

At sixteen years old, Phyllis was a member of the church at the Old South Meeting House. Still possessing the meekness of spirit she always had, she became what many would consider a great writer and an even greater spirit.

*She was very gentle-tempered, extremely affectionate,*
*and altogether free from that most despicable foible,*
*which might naturally have been her besetting sin—*
*literary vanity.*

*We gather from her writings, that she was acquainted*
*with astronomy, ancient and modern geography, and*
*ancient history; and that she was well versed in the*
*scriptures of the Old and New Testament. She discovered*
*a decided taste for the stories of Heathen Mythology,*
*and Pope's Homer seems to have been a great favorite*
*with her.*

*Without any Assistance from School Education, and by*
*only what she was taught in the Family, she, in sixteen*
*Months Time from her Arrival, attained the English*

> *Language, to which she was an utter stranger before, to*
> *such a degree as to read any, the most difficult Parts of*
> *the Sacred Writings, to the great astonishment of all who*
> *heard her.* [44]

Years later, with God's help, Phyllis Wheatley became the first black published author in America. The power that flowed through the pen of Phyllis Wheatley attested to the fact that God was able to penetrate hearts through her, with the ability to make even her enemies her friends. It is written about her, toward the end of her life that:

> *The evidences she has left us of her genius, were the*
> *productions of early and happy days, before her mind*
> *was matured by experience, the depths of her soul*
> *fathomed by suffering, or her fine powers chastened by*
> *affliction. The blight was upon her in her spring-time,*
> *and she passed away.* [45]

## JACKIE ROBINSON—CROSSING THE LINE

*Life is not a spectator sport. If you're going to spend*
*your whole life in the grandstand just watching what*
*goes on, in my opinion you're wasting your life.*

—JACKIE ROBINSON

Amidst racial slurs and angry remarks, the tall, slender athlete stood at the plate waiting for the first pitch. Hopping back from the path of the ball, it seemed that once again the fastball arrived very close to his temple. Another pitch, another near miss—this pattern continued throughout the season.

Such intimidation tactics did not shake the confidence of this future Hall of Fame baseball player. He continued to play, and play greatly. Jackie Robinson had just broken the color barrier in major league baseball.

Robinson was drafted in 1947 from the minor leagues to play for the Brooklyn Dodgers. This seemingly insignificant act was one that divided the country over America's favorite pastime.

A war veteran, only twenty-eight years old, Robinson had played for the Negro league. He was a distinguished citizen and a great athlete. His only fault in the eyes of many was the color of his skin. There were many who applauded his entry into the major leagues, but many players were intimidated by his presence. They purposely tried to hurt him, even injuring him so badly that he walked away from one game with a seven-inch gash on his leg.

Notwithstanding, Robinson was a great player. At bat he was a threat, and he was faster than most, which enabled him to steal bases. His very first season of play showed him to be such a great player that he earned rookie of the year honors. By season's end, Robinson had proven himself, and his very presence on the baseball field showed everyone the equal ability of blacks among whites. This new awareness caused a severe blow to segregationists who believed that blacks had no business playing alongside white ballplayers.

The pressure remained on Robinson. On road games, he could not share hotels with his teammates. He could not eat at restaurants that invited the rest of his fellow players. The star of the Brooklyn Dodgers was often treated poorly by others. Yet he was there and had no plans to leave.

A devout Christian, Robinson often spoke out against the racial injustices of the day. Using his platform as an athlete, he often served as a voice for justice and equality. Even if equality did not exist in his day on the baseball field, he was more than an equal. He triumphed.

He played professional baseball for ten years, with a .311 lifetime batting average. He stole home plate 19 times, won the National League MVP award in 1949, and led the league with a .342 batting average and 37 stolen bases. This Hall of Fame baseball player represented the true potential of blacks physically, mentally, and spiritually.

## LES BROWN—INSPIRER OF DREAMS

*If you take responsibility for yourself you will develop a
hunger to accomplish your dreams.*

—LES BROWN

Not many people embody the ability to personally triumph
over all odds as Les Brown. Adopted as infants in Liberty City,
Miami, Les Brown and his brother, Wes, were raised in the home
of a Godly and caring woman named Mamie Brown.

Mamie Brown had very little formal education and was
poverty-stricken. Many children raised in such an environment
failed in life, ended up in prison, were victimized by street life, or
found an early grave. However, Les Brown triumphed in life and
continues to do so.

In school, Les Brown was labeled a slow learner. He was a
restless, often mischievous student, who could hardly sit in the
same place for more than a few minutes. This label placed upon
him depleted his confidence level, and it took him years to
recover. But he recovered—in a big way.

*Other people's opinion of you does not have to become
your reality.*[46]

This simple statement rang true for Les. He not only rose
above the societal elements of his day; he experienced life as a
three-term legislator, community leader, political activist, and

best-selling author.

He proved that nothing is impossible for any of us—regardless of age, circumstance, or level of financial ability. We can all succeed in life if we will trust in God and face life with personal responsibility.

## SOJOURNER TRUTH—UNBREAKABLE TO ALL BUT GOD

*That little man in black there, he says women can't have as much rights as men, 'cause Christ wasn't a woman! Where did your Christ come from? From God and a woman! Man had nothing to do with him.*

--*AIN'T I A WOMAN?* SPEECH, 1851 WOMEN'S RIGHTS CONVENTION, AKRON, OHIO

*"Who are you?" she exclaimed, as the vision brightened into a form distinct, beaming with the beauty of holiness, and radiant with love. She then said, audibly addressing the mysterious visitant—"I know you, and I don't know you." Meaning, "You seem perfectly familiar; I feel that you not only love me, but that you always have loved me—yet I know you not—I cannot call you by name." When she said, "I know you," the subject of the vision remained distinct and quiet. When she said, "I don't know you," it moved restlessly about, like agitated waters. So while she repeated, without intermission, "I know you, I know you," that the vision might remain— "Who are you?" was the cry of her heart, and her whole soul was in one deep prayer that this heavenly personage might be revealed to her, and remain with her. At length, after bending both soul and body with the intensity of this desire, till breath and strength seemed failing, and she could maintain her position no longer, an answer*

*came to her, saying distinctly, "It is Jesus." "Yes," she
responded, "it is Jesus."*[47]

She knew Him because He came to her. This single experience
with God turned a passionless, backslidden woman into a
firebrand, not just for the struggle for equality for blacks and
women, but also for the Kingdom of God.

Sojourner was actually born into slavery with the name
Isabella. She changed her name after she became convinced that
God had called her into the ministry to travel as a preacher—and
she became Sojourner Truth.

She immediately connected with the abolitionist movement.
She met and worked with Harriet Beecher Stowe, the author of
*Uncle Tom's Cabin,* as well as Frederick Douglass.

So bold was this woman of God that it is said that Frederick
Douglass was a featured speaker at an event, and Truth showed no
reserve in correcting him as he spoke of the helpless conditions of
blacks in America. Events that had occurred at that time in history
had become overwhelming. Douglass even suggested that blacks
needed to take arms and free themselves, which at the time would
clearly have been no match for the powers that enslaved them. As
Douglass spoke of such a hopeless solution, Sojourner simply
raised her voice as he spoke, asking, "Frederick, is God dead?"

Clearly, God was not, and is not, dead. His fire lived in her
heart. His passion moved through her and hit the listeners squarely
between the eyes.

Later, Sojourner Truth began to identify with the women's movement, which was making a consistent rise to public view. Her "Ain't I a Woman" speech became her most famous speech. Part of that speech stated:

> *I have born 13 children*
> *and seen most all sold into slavery*
> *and when I cried out a mother's grief*
> *none but Jesus heard me. . .*
> *and ain't I a woman?*
> *that little man in black there say*
> *a woman can't have as much rights as a man*
> *cause Christ wasn't a woman*
> *Where did your Christ come from?*
> *From God and a woman!*
> *Man had nothing to do with him!*
> *If the first woman God ever made*
> *was strong enough to turn the world*
> *upside down, all alone*
> *together women ought to be able to turn it*
> *rightside up again.*

Sojourner walked alongside the most prominent black leaders of her day and was herself one of them. The commanding voice that came out of her tall, five-foot-eleven frame demanded attention, and that is exactly what it got. In 1864, she got the attention of President Abraham Lincoln. She met privately with him to discuss many of the issues of her day.

Sojourner Truth rose up from being a slave to becoming an activist and preacher with national prominence. She could not read or write. She was also extremely poor. Yet the impact she made in this nation, through her activism, went far beyond her natural means. It was Jesus that met with her. It was Jesus who had called her to do the impossible with the little she had. And it was Jesus who opened the eyes of many to the plight of women and blacks all over the nation.

# RICHARD ALLEN—FOUNDING FATHER OF THE AME CHURCH

*O crucified Jesus in whom I live, and without whom I die; mortify in me all sensual desires, inflame my heart with thy holy love, that I may no longer esteem the vanities of this world, but place my affections entirely on thee.*

*Let my last breath, when my soul shall leave my body, breathe forth love to thee, my God; I entered into life without acknowledging thee, let me therefore finish it in loving thee; O let the last act of life be love, remembering that God is love.*[48]

Richard Allen was born a slave in Philadelphia in 1760. He, along with his mother, father, and siblings were sold to someone else in the state of Delaware, where he stayed until he was about twenty years of age. He was awakened to the fact that he was without a Savior and lost in sin. Shortly after this realization, he obtained God's mercy through the blood of Jesus Christ by accepting Him as Savior and Lord. But not much later, doubts began to rise in his heart.

*I went rejoicing for several days, and was happy in the Lord, in conversing with many old experienced Christians. I was brought under doubts, and was tempted to believe I was deceived, and was constrained*

*to seek the Lord afresh. I went with my head bowed*
*down for many days. My sins were a heavy burden. I*
*was tempted to believe there was no mercy for me. I cried*
*to the Lord both night and day. One night I thought hell*
*would be my portion. I cried unto Him who delighteth to*
*hear the prayers of a poor sinner; and all of a sudden my*
*dungeon shook, my chains flew off, and glory to God, I*
*cried. My soul was filled. I cried, enough for me—the*
*Saviour died. Now my confidence was strengthened that*
*the Lord, for Christ's sake, had heard my prayers, and*
*pardoned all my sins. I was constrained to go from house*
*to house, exhorting my old companions, and telling to all*
*around what a dear Saviour I had found.* [49]

Richard Allen lived with a slaveholder whom he described as
"more like a father to his slaves than anything else. He was a very
tender, humane man." Through a miraculous conversion, his slave
master felt that it was no longer appropriate to hold slaves. So he
allowed Richard Allen and his brother to buy their freedom.

*We left our master's house, and I may truly say it was*
*like leaving our father's house; for he was a kind,*
*affectionate, and tender-hearted master and told us to*
*make his house our home when we were out of a place or*
*sick. While living with him we had family prayer in the*
*kitchen, to which he frequently would come out himself*
*at time of prayer, and my mistress with him. At length*
*he invited us from the kitchen to the parlor to hold*
*family prayer, which we attended too. We had our stated*

*times to hold our prayer meetings and give exhortations
in the neighborhood.*

*I had it often impressed upon my mind that I should one
day enjoy my freedom; for slavery is a bitter pill,
notwithstanding we had a good master. But when we
would think that our day's work was never done, we
often thought that after our master's death we were
liable to be sold to the highest bidder, as he was much in
debt; and thus my troubles were increased, and I was
often brought to weep between the porch and the altar.
But I have had reason to bless my dear Lord that a door
was opened unexpectedly for me to buy my time, and
enjoy my liberty.[50]*

Richard Allen lived with the apparent contradiction of a kind
slave master. Yet, the kindness of the slave master is what gave him
the discipline to pray and seek God growing up. When the day came
for him to be free, he was even offered help, if such help was ever
needed. Still, Richard Allen walked the walk of freedom and did not
look back. He was determined to buy his freedom.

It did not take long for Richard Allen to realize that with
freedom came responsibility. He became a laborer in various places
to earn a living and to pay his master for his freedom. Yet, another
fire continually burned in his heart—the call to preach the gospel.
He often awoke in the midst of the night, preaching and praying as
he awakened. He sought God as he worked at his various jobs—

and experienced the chance to preach and minister as he worked as
a delivery man for a salt company.

Soon, those small opportunities to minister became open
invitations to preach at churches.

> *Many souls were awakened, and cried aloud to the Lord
> to have mercy upon them. I was frequently called upon
> by many inquiring what they should do to be saved. I
> appointed them to prayer and supplication at the throne
> of grace, and to make use of all manner of prayer, and
> pointed them to the invitation of our Lord and Saviour
> Jesus Christ, who has said, "Come unto me, all ye that
> are weary and heavy laden, and I will give you rest."
> Glory be to God! and now I know He was a God at hand
> and left not afar off. . . . It was a time of visitation from
> above.*

> *Many were the slain of the Lord. Seldom did I ever
> experience such a time of mourning and lamentation
> among a people. There were but few coloured people in
> the neighbourhood—the most of my congregation was
> white. Some said, "this man must be a man of God; I
> never heard such preaching before."*[51]

Richard Allen continued his ministry as a traveling preacher.
From his humble beginnings as a slave, he became one of the most
prominent African-American religious leaders of his day.

From a young age, Richard Allen's life was characterized by
unlikely circumstances, such as his slave master investing in his life

and being like a father to him. This love, in a system so evil, illustrates the sovereignty of God. It shows His ability to work through the most challenging and terrible of circumstances in order to raise up a man for His work.

Richard's freedom was eventually purchased, and he continued to minister as a free man. Richard Allen is known as the founder of the African Methodist Episcopal Church, which is today one of the largest African-American ministry organizations in the world.

# BOOKER T. WASHINGTON—ON THE 4TH OF JULY

*As the fireworks light up the sky in celebration of our country's independence this Fourth of July, 1881, I feel my own sense of independence and freedom. It is a reflective day for me, as I think back to the days of my childhood. I wonder what has become of the Burrough family, the master family where I grew up as an unthinkably poor slave. I also wonder whatever became of my father, whom I know nothing of, except that he was a white man.*

*I can still smell the dust of the cabin in which my faithful mother and I lived until we were set free in 1864, thanks to President Lincoln and the end of the Civil War. It was an extremely small log cabin only about 12 feet wide, just enough space to lie down. I slept on a floor made only of dirt, in a bed of rags. Often, during the night I would awaken to see my mother kneeling over me, fervently praying for our freedom. It was her prayers that told me of our prisonhood. For, as a young child, I just thought we were too poor for food or clothes. I did not know of any other type of life, where freedom and choice reigned.*

*After receiving our long sought freedom, my mother, as strict as she was, did her best to raise me a good, honest man. Even though she had never read a book in her life,*

*I know that the lessons of integrity she taught me will last forever. However, I desired something more. As I worked in a salt mine, I dreamed about going to school and learning to read and write. I knew that the ol' mine was not the place for me to stay.*

*Ignorance was becoming more and more a barrier for us as we ventured out to live a free life. I soon became tired of Negroes being taken advantage of because we were uneducated. Few ex-slaves were able to read and write at the time, and this made it so difficult for them to enhance their jobs and their way of living. After being enlightened myself, I became an educator at the Hampton Institute. There, I wanted to prepare other African-American people like myself for a productive life as a citizen in a free country. To do this, I attempted to organize courses that would teach the blacks a trade that they could carry into the workforce. This would open up many more opportunities for them.*

*After leaving the Hampton Institute, I wanted to pursue more ways to enable black people to live a full and educated life. In attempts to spread my faith and hope, I have traveled across the country and spoken up for the black rights. Along my paths I have been privileged to enjoy many of the world leaders including Teddy Roosevelt, J. P. Morgan, and Andrew Carnegie. Giving other people like myself a feeling of worth is what my life is all about.*

This is what leads to my profound sense of freedom inside. Today is the first day of class at the Tuskegee Institute, of which I am the proud founder. I arrived here in Tuskegee only a month ago, with no signs of a school. I know what we now have is not much to boast of, the complete Institute being made up of only two buildings, an old church, and a dilapidated shanty, but I like to refer to them as being "well ventilated," not run down. I have learned that perspective can change a man completely. So, it is not the buildings that give me the feelings of a new independence, it is what they symbolize. In these buildings, colored people can learn to read and write, carry out a skill, and fulfill their dreams. Thirty more Negroes, who were once born as slaves, are enrolled here today, and can now feel what it is like to "know." And as for me, Booker T. Washington, I revitalize my feelings of what it means to be free.[52]

## JOHN JASPER—UNSURPASSED PREACHER

Few of the Negro race are more widely known than the Reverend John Jasper. His fame has spread abroad, even beyond the place where he lived. No stranger visiting Richmond feels that his knowledge of the place and people is complete without learning about this remarkable man. One does not fail to carry away the impression that this was no common character.

Mr. Jasper's very appearance was striking. His tall, commanding form, dignified bearing, and his deep and searching eyes rendered him noticeable in a crowd. He had, too, a half-conscious air of superiority, the natural result of self-knowledge in one endowed with more than ordinary abilities; and, in some indefinable way, he gave one the idea of possessing reserve strength for any emergency liable to arise.

In his presence one felt the force of a mighty will and magnetic power. This contributed, in great measure, to his unbounded sway over the hearts and minds of his many hearers. By the exercise of this power, he bore them along with him, excited their interest in his discourse, aroused their sympathy for his earnest advocacy in the cause he deemed right—even though they, perhaps, dissented from the opinions expressed.

Because John was unskilled in the knowledge of the schools, his language was of the most homely kind. No big, ponderous Latin derivatives constituted his vocabulary; his words were mainly from the good old Anglo-Saxon stock—clear, terse, and forcible. In the aptitude to combine these words to form suggestive images, he has been surpassed by few.

Mr. Jasper possessed marked descriptive powers, a remarkable facility for producing wondrous word-pictures. He made the past present, brought the absent to hand, and gave an awful vividness to the horrors of hell and a perceptible reality to the glories of Heaven.

Not least among the gifts God bestowed upon this sable preacher was his power to move the passions. Of all his powers this was the greatest, and all the other elements of his being contributed to the intensity of this and helped to render it the grand secret of his influence, the chief characteristic of the man. Mr. Jasper moved others because he himself was moved. . . . An impression which some, lacking that subtle spell, would use a vast array of words vainly striving to produce, he, with a soul stirred in deep emotion, would oftentimes effect by means of a single epithet. Believing firmly in the truth of his own utterances, courageously advancing independent opinions, he had in his style the added charm of earnestness and originality. He felt, and he showed that he felt. He exhibited a concern for those whom he addressed; he appealed to their interests, to their affections, to their convictions of duty. With a keen insight into human nature, he was able to touch the mainsprings of action, to play with artistic skill upon the feelings. God preeminently gave him the power to lead and persuade the people.

Mr. Jasper was not an educated man; he lacked the advantages of systematic training. That lack of education was his misfortune, and not his fault. That barbarous institution which did all it could to dwarf the black man by stupendous efforts to hinder the progress of superior minds when they dwelt under dark skins, had, among its infinity of infamous results, to answer for the wrong it did to this man of wonderful gifts. Had he been born and reared amid favoring circumstances, he would undoubtedly have been one of the great men of his race, of his calling, of his country. Though the diamond was not under the hand of the polisher, yet we recognize and value it as a jewel most precious in the sight of God.[53]

## JOHN B. MEACHUM—ADVANCING THE RACE THROUGH RIGHTEOUSNESS

*If UNION is God Almighty's plan, let us hasten to it.
The blessing of God will rest upon us. But we may reject
the council of the Father of Light and Knowledge to our
hurt.*

—JOHN MEACHUM

[I] *was born a slave, in Goochland county, Virginia, May
3rd, 1789. I belonged to a man by the name of Paul
Meachum, who moved to North Carolina, and lived
there nine years. He then moved to Hardin county,
Kentucky, where I still remained a slave with him. He
was a good man and I loved him, but could not feel
myself satisfied, for he was very old, and looked as if
death was drawing near to him. So I proposed to him to
hire my time, and he granted it. By working in a
saltpetre cave I earned enough to purchase my freedom.*

*Still I was not satisfied, for I had left my father in old
Virginia, and he was a slave. It seemed to me, at times,
though I was seven hundred miles from him, that I held
conversation with him, for he was near my heart.
However this did not stop here, for industry will do a
great deal. In a short time I went to Virginia, and
bought my father, and paid one hundred pounds for him,
Virginia money. It was a joyful meeting when we met
together, for we had been apart a long time. He was a*

*Baptist preacher, living in Hanover county, and went by
the name of Thomas Granger. While there, on a Sunday
morning after I had bought the old man, he was singing
and my eyes filled with tears. He turned to me and said,
"you are yet in your sins." His words went to my heart,
and I began to pray and seek the Lord. Four weeks from
that day I found peace in believing upon the Lord Jesus,
related my experience to the church, and was baptized by
elder Purinton, in Louisa county. This was in the year
1811, when I was about twenty-one years old. My father
and myself then earned enough to pay our expenses on
the way, and putting our knapsacks on our backs walked
seven hundred miles to Hardin county, Kentucky. Here
the old man met his wife and all his children, who had
been there several years. Oh there was joy!*

*In a short time, my mother and all her children received
their liberty, of their good old master. My father and his
family settled in Harrison county, Indiana.*

*I married a slave in Kentucky, whose master soon took
her to St. Louis, in Missouri. I followed her, arriving
there in 1815, with three dollars in my pocket. Being a
carpenter and cooper I soon obtained business, and
purchased my wife and children. Since that period, I
have purchased about twenty slaves, most of whom paid
back the greatest part of the money, and some paid all.
They are all free at this time, and doing well, excepting
one, who happened to be a drunkard, and no drunkard
can do well. One of the twenty colored friends that I*

*bought is worthy to be taken notice of, to show what industry will do. I paid for him one thousand dollars. He worked and paid back the thousand dollars. He has also bought a lot of ground for which he paid a thousand dollars. He married a slave and bought her, and paid seven hundred dollars for her. He has built a house that cost him six hundred dollars. He is a blacksmith, and has worked for one man ever since he has been in St. Louis. So much for industry.*

*I commenced preaching in 1821, and was ordained as a minister of the gospel in 1825. From that time to this, I have been the pastor of the African Baptist Church in St. Louis, which has now more than five hundred members. The Sunday school has an attendance from one hundred and fifty to three hundred.*[54]

John B. Meachum believed that unity, coupled with a committed relationship with God, was the only way that blacks would be able to advance in America. In his Address to the Colored Citizens of the United States, he wrote:

*Our people can only distinguish themselves as a nation by "fearing God," and "working righteousness," for "righteousness exalteth a nation, but sin is a reproach to any people." We must therefore be united in love and affection—our interests, aims, and hopes must be one— for in the language of the text, "Behold how good and how pleasant it is for brethren to dwell together in*

unity!" We must culivate all the Christian graces which
the apostle Peter recommends—"add to your faith
virtue, and to virtue knowledge, and to knowledge
temperance, and to temperance patience, and to patience
godliness, and to godliness brotherly kindness, and to
brotherly kindness charity." Upon the exercise of these
graces and christian qualities depend our elevation in
this life, and our eternal happiness in the world to come.

We must have union—we can and must have it, else we
shall remain in darkness, ignorance and superstition, in
a state of moral and intellectual degradation. It is an old
maxim with which you are all familiar—"in union there
is strength." Again, "united we stand, divided we fall."
Let us then be of one mind, and one spirit, and cultivate
that principle of true benevolence which will exert a
wholesome and salutary influence on the world, secure
the blessings of God upon us, and benefit our own souls.[55]

———∞∞∞———

## CONDOLEEZA RICE—FIRST BLACK NATIONAL SECURITY ADVISOR

Less than 150 years after the signing of the Emancipation Proclamation, the class of people once slaves has moved farther ahead than any other formally enslaved race in modern history. Condoleeza Rice, the first black (male or female) National Security Advisor, is a testament to this fact.

As far as national security is concerned, there is perhaps only one person who is more powerful than Doctor Rice, and that one person is the President of the United States.

Rice entered the University of Denver at the age of fifteen, graduating at only nineteen years old with a bachelor's degree in political science. She also earned a master's degree at the University of Notre Dame and a Ph.D. from the University of Denver's Graduate School of International Studies.

Working for years as an award-winning professor, Condoleeza Rice continued her career in the George H. W. Bush Sr. administration as Director, and then Senior Director, of Soviet and East European Affairs in the National Security Council, and as a Special Assistant to the President for National Security Affairs.

While her entire story has not yet been told, her influence up to this point has been phenomenal. She played a major role in the Cold War and continues to hold a key role in securing the United States in the war on terror in both Afghanistan and Iraq.

Doctor Rice clearly shows just how far black America has come for those who have seized the opportunity that was fought for years earlier. Her success is a testimony to the fact that God indeed had the African American in mind when Nehemiah raised his voice, proclaiming, *"The God of heaven, he will prosper us; therefore we his servants will arise and build"* (Nehemiah 2:20 KJV).

# THOMAS LEWIS JOHNSON—MISSIONARY TO AFRICA

*These people can talk to each other on their drums
almost as well as we can send a message in this country
by telegraph. They have schools in which to teach their
children this drum-beating telegraphy. On this occasion
this man said on his drum, "White man come into our
country." The natives with us, twelve in number, did not
tell me of this till the next day.*

*On Saturday morning at nine o'clock, as we were taking
our breakfast on the river bank, several canoes passed
us, with fifteen to twenty men in each. Seeing they were
well armed with guns and cutlasses, we began to feel
suspicious. About ten o'clock we came up with them.
They had all stopped on the bank, put on their war caps,
and stood in a line along the river.*

*We were ordered to come ashore. We told them we would
not. If they had anything to say to us they must come out
in their canoes. They tried to make us leave our boat and
go on the beach, but we resolved to stay in our boat. I do
not know of any time in my life when I realised the
precious promise of my blessed Jesus more than in this
hour, "Lo, I am with you alway," I said to my wife and
her sister, Mrs. Richardson, "We lean upon the Lord."*

*At one time we were surrounded by nearly one hundred
men, armed with cutlasses, ready to cut into us as soon*

*as the young prince gave the word of command. We soon found that it was impossible for us to proceed.*[56]

The band of missionaries to Africa was imprisoned, but soon were granted freedom in exchange for various goods that they kept on them. From there, they continued in their work for God. Numbered among them was a young missionary by the name of Thomas Johnson.

Thomas Johnson was born in 1836 at Rock-Rayman in the state of Virginia. He was the child of slaves, and he spent his entire childhood as a slave. Yet, this did not keep him from his destiny.

It was not until the end of the Civil War that Thomas Johnson would ever be able to consider himself free, at least as far as his physical state was concerned. He documented the day he found out that the Confederate capital had fallen:

*The joy and rejoicing of the coloured people when the United States army marched into Richmond defies description. For days the manifestations of delight were displayed in many ways. The places of worship were kept open, and hundreds met for prayer and praise. Of the many songs of the Jubilee this was the chorus of one of them:*

> *Slavery's chain is broke at last,*
> *Broke at last, broke at last;*
> *Slavery's chain is broke at last,*
> *I'm going to praise God till I die.*

*I cannot now describe the joy of my soul at that time.*
*This was indeed the third birthday to me:*
*Born August 7th, 1836—a "Thing."*
*Born again (John 3:7), June, 1857—a Child of God.*
*Born into human liberty, April 3rd, 1865—a Free Man.*

*No longer was I a mere chattel, but a man, free in body,*
*free in soul; praise the Lord. It is impossible to give an*
*adequate idea of the abounding joy of the people—the*
*great multitude of liberated slaves—after the long years*
*of toil and suffering. Strong men and women were*
*weeping and praising God at the same time. Those who*
*were not Christians exhibited their joy in other ways.*
*They capered about and beat their banjos; some of them*
*climbed up trees and yelled out expressions of wild*
*delight, and others made speeches to the crowds. That*
*scene of years ago comes up vividly before me at this*
*moment. The long night of affliction in the house of our*
*bondage had passed, and that deeply desired and hoped*
*for and prayed for time had come! The cries and groans*
*and prayers of millions of poor and defenceless slaves,*
*with the prayers of their friends in America, England,*
*Ireland, Scotland, Wales, and everywhere, had reached*
*the throne of God. Innocent blood of murdered men and*
*women and children had cried unto God from the*
*ground, and He in His own time, which is always the*
*right time and best time, and in His own way, which is*
*the very best way, answered that cry.*[57]

Upon entering freedom, Thomas Johnson worked numerous jobs in order to support himself, but his heart was to do the work of God. Many temptations came to him in order to hinder his fulfillment of God's calling, including the temptation of money. He did not answer to those temptations, but instead stayed his course and began to pastor a church in Denver. Yet, there was still a yearning in his heart.

> *During all this time I could not lose sight of Africa. Many of those to whom I would make known my desires sought to dissuade me from my purpose, telling me of what they had read and heard of Africa and its venomous reptiles, cruel fevers and cannibal tribes. But these things did not move me. There were times when I would seriously consider the question of health and other matters; but there was something which kept Africa continually before me with its great need of the Gospel; and I was concerned about my preparation to go and tell the people the good news of the Gospel of Jesus Christ. I was told that I must be educated before I could be sent as a missionary. I earnestly prayed over the matter; and I begged the Lord that if it were His will, He would send me to Africa to open up the way.* [58]

God eventually opened up the way, and he was able to begin his missionary journey to Africa. And while his fathers had left Africa in chains, he was able to return, taking freedom and the light of the glorious gospel of Christ to many.

# MARTIN LUTHER KING JR.—THE EXTREMIST FOR LOVE

*We must learn to live together as brothers or perish together as fools.*

—MARTIN LUTHER KING JR.

His spirit was invigorated by the soulful singing of Mahalia Jackson before 250,000 people at the Lincoln Memorial. Their hearts were charged, waiting to hear something that would change the way America viewed them in their struggle. People from all over the country, including media and law enforcement, had awaited the moment when Doctor Martin Luther King would make the most important speech of his life.

It was during late summer in 1963 when Dr. King would share his dream:

*"I have a dream that one day the state of Alabama, whose governor's lips are presently dripping with the words of interposition and nullification, will be transformed into a situation where little black boys and black girls will be able to join hands with little white boys and white girls and walk together as sisters and brothers. I have a dream today. I have a dream that one day every valley shall be exalted, every hill and mountain shall be made low, the rough places will be made plain, and the crooked places will be made straight, and the glory of the Lord shall be revealed, and*

all flesh shall see it together. This is our hope. This is the
faith with which I return to the South. With this faith we
will be able to hew out of the mountain of despair a
stone of hope. With this faith we will be able to
transform the jangling discords of our nation into a
beautiful symphony of brotherhood. With this faith we
will be able to work together, to pray together, to struggle
together, to go to jail together, to stand up for freedom
together, knowing that we will be free one day.

"This will be the day when all of God's children will be
able to sing with a new meaning, 'My country, 'tis of
thee, sweet land of liberty, of thee I sing. Land where my
fathers died, land of the pilgrim's pride, from every
mountainside, let freedom ring.' And if America is to be
a great nation, this must become true. So let freedom
ring from the prodigious hilltops of New Hampshire. Let
freedom ring from the mighty mountains of New York.
Let freedom ring from the heightening Alleghenies of
Pennsylvania! Let freedom ring from the snowcapped
Rockies of Colorado! Let freedom ring from the
curvaceous peaks of California! But not only that; let
freedom ring from Stone Mountain of Georgia! Let
freedom ring from Lookout Mountain of Tennessee! Let
freedom ring from every hill and every molehill of
Mississippi. From every mountainside, let freedom ring.

"When we let freedom ring, when we let it ring from
every village and every hamlet, from every state and
every city, we will be able to speed up that day when all
of God's children, black men and white men, Jews and

> *Gentiles, Protestants and Catholics, will be able to join*
> *hands and sing in the words of the old Negro spiritual,*
> *'Free at last! Free at last! Thank God Almighty, we are*
> *free at last!'"*[59]

At that moment, history was made. No records were broken that day. Neither had any legislation been passed. This was the day when it became clear that African Americans were not going to be stopped until every sign of legalized segregation in America was nullified.

Martin Luther King was only 34 years old. But the power of his convictions went far beyond his years. He endured assaults, arrests, and fierce criticism from media outlets as well as individuals who felt that he was a threat to the normalcy of his time. Even some church leaders felt that he was fanatical about his cause, to which he responded:

> *But though I was initially disappointed at being*
> *categorized as an extremist, as I continued to think*
> *about the matter I gradually gained a measure of*
> *satisfaction from the label. Was not Jesus an extremist*
> *for love: "Love your enemies, bless them that curse you,*
> *do good to them that hate you, and pray for them which*
> *despitefully use you, and persecute you." Was not Amos*
> *an extremist for justice: "Let justice roll down like waters*
> *and righteousness like an ever-flowing stream." Was not*
> *Paul an extremist for the Christian gospel: "I bear in my*
> *body the marks of the Lord Jesus." Was not Martin*

> *Luther an extremist: "Here I stand; I cannot do*
> *otherwise, so help me God." And John Bunyan: "I will*
> *stay in jail to the end of my days before I make a*
> *butchery of my conscience." And Abraham Lincoln:*
> *"This nation cannot survive half slave and half free."*
> *And Thomas Jefferson: "We hold these truths to be self-*
> *evident, that all men are created equal ..." So the*
> *question is not whether we will be extremists, but what*
> *kind of extremists we will be. Will we be extremists for*
> *hate or for love?*[60]

It is clear what Martin Luther King's answer was. His "extreme" approach to the cause of justice cost him his life. He was assasinated in a hotel in Memphis, outside on his balcony. But his death did not stop the cause for freedom. He was a victor in life and in death. Forever, African Americans owe their gratitude to the fiery commitment of a man who dared to lift up his voice and speak against injustice—in the name of God.

# HARRIET TUBMAN—THE FIELD HAND REDEEMER

*"I had reasoned this out in my mind, there was one of two things I had a right to, liberty or death; if I could not have one, I would have the other."*

--HARRIET TUBMAN

The small group of fugitives huddled in the night, waiting for their next move. They had to hurry. They would soon be chased by those who wished to recapture them and bring them back into slavery. The mission was treacherous, but it had to be done. In this situation, the words of Patrick Henry were clear, "Give me liberty, or give me death." They had in a way chosen both, and they were led by a woman who could assure them of neither one.

If there were any who were of a faint heart and wished to go back, they would never make it alive. This was from the mouth of a woman called Moses. Her real name was Harriet Tubman. Her tenacity was so strong that she carried a pistol reserved for any who decided that they preferred the life of a slave, as opposed to the life of a fugitive, or a free man. The mission was truly life or death. Through her determination, she never lost a passenger. They all survived and made it to freedom in the North.

Harriet Tubman also fought in the Civil War, helping the Union soldiers as a spy, nurse, scout, and soldier. Her life belonged to her cause—freedom. Her every breath seemed to desire to do more for the sake of her fellow kinsmen and women.

She was born a slave in Maryland, under severe circumstances. She was a field hand, often beaten, and suffered many of the atrocities that female slaves faced at the hands of their owners. Yet nothing stopped her heart from looking toward the star of freedom—the North Star. This was her guide as she escaped to the North and served as guide for over 300 slaves escaping to the North through the underground railroad.

Harriet Tubman's story has become legendary. Unlike most legends, her story was true and many are indebted to her courage and strive for freedom.

## COLIN POWELL—SOLDIER FOR LIFE

Luther and Maud Powell had a son on April 5th, 1937. In the face of extreme financial and economic challenges, there were not many opportunities for black Jamaican immigrants in the poverty-stricken South Bronx, New York. But the child in the arms of Maud Powell would become one of the most powerful men on earth. They named him Colin.

In his early years he went to public school and later attended City College in New York City. He participated in ROTC and experienced his first taste of military life. After graduating from college, Colin joined the army immediately, where he served for the next 35 years. He achieved the rank of a four-star general.

Military life was *his* life. "The discipline, the structure, the camaraderie, the sense of belonging were what I craved," he wrote, comparing [military life] to the other pillar of his life, the Episcopal church.[61]

Following a distinguished military career, he began an organization called America's Promise. This organization was derived from five promises that Powell felt every child needed—caring adults, safe places, a healthy start, marketable skills, and opportunities to serve. His organization thrived for years, and he worked diligently to see it come into full fruition. Then, one of the most important calls of his life came.

Following a much-contested and controversial election, the

newly elected President George W. Bush called him to be the Secretary of State. His distinguished career and his history as a leader earned him the privilege of becoming Secretary of State. No African American has ever held such a high office. Through years of service and sacrifice, Colin Powell earned this extremely important position. He was unanimously confirmed by an extremely divided Senate and began serving in December of 2000.

His leadership has served America in times of war and peace. He continues to play a vital role in the war on terror. A young black child in the streets of the South Bronx became the international face of America. When he speaks, the nations of the world take notice. A love for God and a determination to rise out of poverty and despair pulled Colin Powell from the ghetto to the seat of power.

## JAMES DERHAM—PHYSICIAN SLAVE

James Durham started out as a slave and later became a respected physician. Although honored and revered in literature and by word-of-mouth, most of Derham's contributions are now forever lost in history. But many of his successes were written of by Wilson Armistead:

*He was a descendant of Africa, originally a Slave in Philadelphia, was sold to a medical man, who employed him as an assistant in the preparation of drugs. During the American war he was sold to a surgeon, and by him to Dr. Dove, of New Orleans. He learned the English, French, and Spanish languages, so as to speak them with ease.*

*He was received a member of the English church; and in 1788, when about 21 years of age, he became one of the most distinguished physicians at New Orleans. "I conversed with him on medicine," says Dr. Rush, "and found him very learned. I thought I could give him information concerning the treatment of diseases; but I learned more from him than he could expect from me."*

*The Pennsylvania Society, established in favour of the people of Colour, thought it their duty, in 1789, to publish these facts; which are also related by Dickson. In the Domestic Medicine of Buchan, and in a work of Duplaint, we find an account of a cure for the bite of a rattlesnake. It is not clear whether Derham was the discoverer; but it is a well known fact, that, for this important discovery, we are indebted to one of his Colour, who received his freedom from the general assembly of Carolina, and also an annuity of one-hundred pounds.*[62]

James Durham was America's first black physician, yet he never went to medical school. During his life he was owned by three different doctors and had acquired so much knowledge that his third owner suggested that he begin to practice medicine. So willing was James to start his own practice that he opened his practice in New Orleans at only 26 years old, and earned over $3,000 a year, a huge sum of money during the 18th Century.

It is not clear whether or not he was ever freed, but despite his living conditions at the time, his life of learning and service was an inspiration to black physicians who came after him.

# JAMES W.C. PENNINGTON—FROM SERVANT OF MAN TO SERVANT OF GOD

Another savage whipping drove into James the resolve to finally escape the cruel home of a blacksmith to whom his parents were also slaves. He followed the North Star to freedom. His journey was not an easy one—he was captured and escaped twice. He made his way to Pennsylvania, where eventually James would breathe the air of freedom in the home of a Quaker. It was here that he began his formal education. He was 20 years old.

He later relocated to New York, where he met a Presbyterian minister who mentored him. James began to learn about the teachings and life of Jesus. He was never the same after experiencing so great a salvation.

> *The fugitive first found a shelter at the house of a Friend in Pennsylvania, with whom he remained six months. "It was while living with this Friend," he observed, "and by his kind attention in teaching me, that I acquired my first knowledge of writing, arithmetic, and geography." In these he made rapid progress during the six months, at the expiration of which, it became necessary for his safety to remove further north, to be more out of the reach of menstealers. He therefore removed to Long Island. Here, he soon felt the loss of his kind Friend and tutor, but he was successful in obtaining employment, and remained in the service of one gentleman for three*

*years, during the whole of which period his scanty leisure was closely occupied in study.*

*Pennington had so far improved himself at the expiration of five years from the time of his escape from Slavery, that an application was made to him, to teach a small school of Coloured children, at New Town, near Flushing, on Long-Island. Being previously examined by a committee, his services were accepted, and he taught the school successfully for two years.*

With a strong desire to serve God more deeply, James Pennington began to study at a theological seminary. In time, he became a professor at this seminary and began to minister the gospel.

At a time when he could have been spiteful concerning those outside of his own race, he was gracious and open. Pennington started a church, which grew to a flourishing congregation. He soon became a member and president of the Hatford Central Association of Congregational Ministers, which was an assembly composed entirely of whites.

At this assembly, two young men presented themselves before him, asking that they might be licensed to the ministry. They, too, were white. After rigorous testing he was able to license and certify two white candidates for the ministry—one of whom was from Kentucky, a slave state.

James W. C. Pennington later began publishing his own works, such as "A Text of the Origin and History of the Coloured People," and "An Address on West India Emancipation." He bravely refuted the notion that blacks were inferior to whites, and his life proved it.[63]

# LOTT CAREY—BLACK AFRICAN MISSIONARY

This self-taught African was born a slave near Richmond,
Virginia. He was the only child of parents, themselves slaves, who
were of a pious turn of mind; and though he had no instruction from
books, the admonitions of his father and mother may have laid the
foundations of his future usefulness. In 1804, the young slave was
sent to Richmond and hired out as a common laborer at a
warehouse in the place.

He was excessively profane and much addicted to intoxication;
but God was pleased to awaken him to a sense of his sinfulness. He
happened to hear a sermon, and he desired to be able to read,
chiefly with a view of becoming acquainted with the nature of
certain transactions recorded in the New Testament. He obtained a
Bible and began to learn his letters by trying to read the chapter he
had heard illustrated in the sermon. With a little perseverance and
assistance, he was able to read. This acquisition created in him a
desire to write, an accomplishment he soon also mastered.

He became more useful to his employers by being able to check
and superintend the shipping of tobacco. In time he saved 850
dollars and with the money purchased his freedom and that of two
of his children.

"Of the real value of his services while in his employment,"
says an American writer, "no one but a dealer in tobacco can form
an idea. Notwithstanding the hundreds of hogsheads which were

committed to his charge, he could produce any one the moment it was called for; and the shipments were made with a promptness and correctness such as no person, white or black, has equaled in the same situation. The last year in which he remained in the warehouse, his salary was 800 dollars, and he might have received a larger sum, if he would have continued."

For his ability in his work, besides being highly esteemed by his master, he was frequently rewarded by the merchant with a five-dollar note. He was allowed to sell, for his own benefit, small parcels of damaged tobacco. It was by saving the little sums obtained in this way and with the aid of subscriptions by the merchants to whose interests he had been attentive that he was enabled to purchase the freedom of his family. He also bought a house and some land in Richmond, and when the colonists were fitted out for Africa, he was enabled to bear a considerable part of his own expenses.

Soon after making a profession of religion, Lott Carey commenced holding meetings and exhorting the colored people; and, though he had little knowledge of books, or acquaintance with mankind, he frequently exhibited a boldness of thought and a strength of native intellect which no acquirement could have given him. While employed at the warehouse, he devoted his leisure time to reading such books as accident threw in his way. It is said that a gentleman, on one occasion, taking up a volume which he had left for a few moments, found it to be Smith's "Wealth of Nations."

As early as 1815, Lott Carey began to feel special interest in the cause of African missions and contributed probably more than any other person in giving origin and character to the African Missionary Society established that year in Richmond. His benevolence was practical, and whenever and wherever good objects were to be effected, he was ready to lend his aid. He was among the earliest emigrants to Africa.

At the close of his farewell sermon in the first Baptist meeting house in the city before his departure, he remarked as follows:

*I am about to leave you; and expect to see your faces no more. I long to preach to the poor African the way of life and salvation. I do not know what may befall me, whether I may find a grave in the ocean, or among savage men, or more savage wild beasts on the coast of Africa; nor am I anxious what may become of me. I feel it my duty to go; and I very much fear, that many of those who preach the gospel in this country, will blush when the Saviour calls them to give an account of their labors in his cause, and tells them, "I commanded you to go into all the world, and preach the gospel to every creature:" (and with the most forcible emphasis he exclaimed:) the Saviour may ask—"Where have you been? What have you been doing? Have you endeavored to the utmost of your ability to fulfill the commands I gave you—or have you sought your own gratification and your own ease, regardless of my commands?"[64]*

Being twice married, he lost his second wife shortly after arriving at Sierra Leone. Of her triumphant death, he gives a most affecting account in his journal of that date. On his arrival in Africa, Lott Carey saw before him a wide and interesting field, demanding various and powerful talents and the most devoted piety. His intellectual ability, firmness of purpose, unbending integrity, correct judgment, and disinterested benevolence, soon placed him in a conspicuous station and gave him a wide and commanding influence. Though naturally diffident and retiring, his worth was too evident to allow for his remaining in obscurity.

An American writer, in speaking of this intelligent Negro about this period of his life, makes the following observations:

> *Lott Carey is now more than forty years of age. He is possessed of a constitution peculiarly fitted for toil and exposure; and has felt the effects of climate perhaps less than any other individual on the Cape. He has always shown that sort of inflexible integrity and correctness of deportment towards all which necessarily commands respect; but he will probably never be able to divest himself of a kind of suspicious reserve towards white people, especially his superiors, which universally attaches itself to those reared in slavery. The interests of the colonies, and the cause of his countrymen, both in Africa, and in this country, lie near his heart. For them he is willing to toil, and to make almost any sacrifice; and he has frequently declared, that nothing could induce him to return.* [65]

The peculiar exposure of the early emigrants, the scantiness of their supplies, and the want of adequate medical attention subjected them to severe sufferings. To relieve these conditions, Lott Carey obtained all the information in his power concerning the diseases of the climate and the proper remedies. He made liberal sacrifices of his property on behalf of the poor and distressed, and devoted his time almost exclusively to their relief. His services as a physician to the colony were invaluable and were long rendered without hope of reward.

He was made Health Officer and General Inspector of the Settlement of Monrovia, but he refused for some time to accept any other civil office. During the sickly season of the year, he was mostly occupied in attending the sick, having no other physician among them. But amidst his multiplied cares and efforts for the colony, he never neglected to promote civilization and Christianity among the natives.

In 1826, Carey was elected vice-agent of the colony and discharged the duties of that important office till his death, which occurred in 1828 in the most melancholy manner. One evening, while he and several others were engaged in making cartridges to defend the colony against a slave-trader, a candle was accidentally overturned, which ignited some powder, producing an explosion that resulted in the death of eight people. Carey survived for two days. Such was the unfortunate death of this active colored apostle of civilization on the coast of Africa, where his memory will long be cherished. The career which he pursued and the intelligence which marked his character testify that the race of blacks is not destitute of moral worth and innate genius, and that their culture would liberally produce an abundant harvest of the best principles and those results which dignify human nature.[66]

## CORNELIUS—MISSIONARY IN ST. THOMAS

In 1801, the mission of the Moravians in the Danish island of St. Thomas was deprived of one of its most intelligent and useful native assistants, who for more than fifty years had walked worthy of his calling by the Gospel—the Negro Cornelius, a man in many respects distinguished among his countrymen.

About the year 1750, Cornelius became concerned for the salvation of his soul and felt a strong impulse to attend the preaching of the missionaries and their private instructions. Being baptized, he ever after remained faithful to the grace conferred upon him. He had a humble and growing sense of the depravity of his heart and made daily progress in the knowledge of Christ.

He was blessed with a good natural understanding and, having learned the business of a mason, received the appointment of master-mason to the royal buildings, in which employment he was esteemed by all who knew him as a clever, upright, and disinterested man. He laid the foundation of six chapels belonging to the mission in the Danish islands. He was able to write and speak the Creole, Dutch, Danish, German, and English languages. Until 1767, he was a slave in the royal plantation, afterwards belonging to Count Schimmelman. He first purchased the freedom of his wife and then labored hard to gain his own liberty, which he effected after much entreaty and the payment of a considerable ransom. God blessed him and the work of his hands in such a manner that he also purchased by degrees the emancipation of his six children.

In 1754, he was appointed assistant in the mission. After his emancipation, he greatly exerted himself in the service of the Lord, especially among the people of his own color, and spent whole days and nights in visiting them. He possessed a peculiar talent for expressing his ideas with great clearness, which rendered his discourse pleasing and edifying to white people as well as to Negroes. Yet he was by no means elated by the talents he possessed. His character was that of a humble servant of Christ, who thought too meanly of himself to treat others with contempt. To distribute to the indigent and assist the feeble was the delight of his heart, and those he helped always found in him a generous and sympathizing friend and faithful adviser.

While zealously exerting himself in promoting the welfare of his countrymen, he did not neglect the concerns of his family. As arduous as he was in caring for their temporal prosperity by working diligently to purchase their freedom, he was even more adamant in pursuing the welfare of their souls. God blessed his instructions, and Cornelius had the joy of seeing his whole family share in the salvation of the Lord. Being found faithful, they were employed as assistants in the mission.

The infirmities of age increasing upon him, Cornelius ardently longed to depart and be with Christ. A constant cough and pain in his side damped his great activity, caused occasional dejection of

mind, and seemed at times to shake his faith and fortitude. He now
and then complained of a declension of his love to Jesus; and once,
while meditating on that text, "I have somewhat against thee,
because thou hast left thy first love," he exclaimed, "Ah! I too have
left my first love!" A few days before his end, being visited by one of
the missionaries, he said, "I ought to have done more and loved and
served my Saviour better. Yet I firmly trust that He will receive me
in mercy, for I come to Him as a poor sinner, having nothing to
plead but His grace, and righteousness through His blood." With
his children and several of his grandchildren assembled round his
bed, he addressed them in a very solemn and impressive manner to
the following effect:

> *I rejoice exceedingly, my dearly beloved children, to see
> you once more together before my departure, for I believe
> that my Lord and Saviour will soon come and take your
> father home to himself. You know, dear children, what
> my chief concern has been respecting you, as long as I
> was with you; how frequently I have exhorted you not to
> neglect the day of grace, but to surrender yourselves with
> soul and body to your Redeemer, and to follow Him
> faithfully. My dear children, attend to my last wish and
> dying request. Love one another! Do not suffer any
> quarrels and disputes to arise among you after my
> decease. No, my children, raising his voice, love one
> another cordially: let each strive to shew proofs of love to
> his brother or sister; nor suffer yourselves to be tempted
> by anything to become proud, for by that you may even*

*miss of your soul's salvation, but pray our Saviour to grant you lowly minds and humble hearts. If you follow this advice of your father's, my joy will be complete, when I shall once see you all again in eternal bliss, and be able to say to our Saviour—Here, Lord, is thy poor unworthy Cornelius, and the children Thou hast given me. I am sure our Saviour will not forsake you; but, I beseech You, do not forsake Him.*

Cornelius fell gently asleep in Jesus on the twenty-ninth of November, being about 84 years of age.[67]

## ARTHUR ASHE—THE CHAMPION

*From what we get, we can make a living; what we give,
however, makes a life.*

— ARTHUR ASHE

In the midst of a distinguished career in the United States, the
number one ranked American athlete tennis player and one of the
world's best athletes, applied for a visa to South Africa to play in
the South African Open. The South African Open was among the
most prestigious events in the country and was certain to expand
the international fame of this young champion. His visa was
rejected in 1969, not because he was a criminal or an international
threat. It was rejected because of the color of his skin.

Rather than cower in the face of the racist political policies of
South Africa, the devout Christian called for the removal of South
Africa from the tennis tour. That request was accepted, and the
backlash against South Africa was harsh. The evil of the system of
apartheid was exposed in an even greater manner than it had been
previously. Because of the bold stand of this young man, South
African blacks began to witness the process of change in their
country that would soon grow into freedom and equality.

This stand exemplified the nature of Arthur Ashe—one of the
greatest tennis players ever to take the court. From there, Ashe
became an outspoken critic of the system of apartheid, openly

supporting the nation's most prominent political prisoner at the time, the future South African president, Nelson Mandela. Ashe instantly won great prominence among blacks in America and abroad.

Arthur Ashe Jr. was born in Richmond, Virginia, in 1943. He began playing tennis at the age of seven. Then, in his preteen years, he attracted the attention of a tennis coach who chose to connect Ashe with the more prominent tennis coach Walter Johnson. Johnson had coached tennis great Althea Gibson. He became Ashe's mentor. This journey propelled Arthur Ashe to become one of the world's greatest athletes.

Years later, as a student at UCLA, he became the first African-American player to be named to the United States Davis Cup team. After graduating from UCLA with a business degree, he continued playing as an amateur until he won the U. S. Open in 1968. From there, the champion in Ashe began to shine, and he later won the Australian Open and Wimbledon. Ashe retired after a distinguished career of 818 wins and 51 titles, and was inducted into the Tennis Hall of Fame in 1980.

Health problems, including a heart attack, forced his retirement. In retirement, Ashe served as a spokesperson for the American Heart Association and consistently spoke out against the evils of apartheid in South Africa. He also served as a commentator, sports writer, and mentor to young people in the game of tennis.

In 1983 he needed heart surgery. Shortly after the surgery, he was given a blood transfusion which contained blood that had been contaminated with HIV. He dedicated the remainder of his life to AIDS education, even addressing the UN General Assembly in 1992. At forty-nine years old, he died of AIDS-related illnesses.

Though his death was untimely, Arthur Ashe's life was glorious. In a time of deep racial segregation and bitterness, Arthur knew how to walk in love and dignity. To the very end, he looked a challenge eye-to-eye and challenged it to a duel. And in the end, Ashe always emerged as the victor. History will always remember him as one of the greatest tennis players who ever lived.

# E. V. Hill—Strength in Humility

*When I come to the end of my journey—when my sun goes down. When it is all over, when my work on earth is done—I have God and the place He has prepared for me. I have a glorious sunset.*[68]

--E.V. Hill

He picked cotton, raised hogs, harvested peanuts, and inaugurated a President of the United States—all in one lifetime. He served as a healing voice in the aftermath of the L.A. riots, ministered in citywide evangelistic outreaches, and served in numerous presidential administrations. He was a policy adviser for the Los Angeles County mayor. These diverse accomplishments were all fulfilled by Edward Victor Hill, Pastor of Mount Zion Missionary Baptist Church.

E.V. Hill was born in 1933 in Columbus, Texas. Although his beginnings were humble, he was not ashamed of them. According to him, there was nothing embarrassing about a lack of certain luxuries in life, as very few of the people he knew as a child had them.

E.V. Hill was a man who magnified the Savior. More than anything, his desire was to bring people to a saving knowledge of Jesus Christ. This idea was central to all that he did, whether political or religious.

*Wherever you go, no matter what class—whether it's*

*politicians, seminarians, professors, teachers, or even*
*with people whose homes are breaking up—the heart's*
*plea is, "I need a Savior."*[69]

This was the heart of the message of E.V. Hill—the need for a Savior. Often appearing on Christian television, Hill was among the first African-American preachers to gain national prominence over the airwaves. It was on television that he was able to minister his message of God's saving power to millions of people worldwide. In the end, over 25,000 people were introduced to the Savior through E.V. Hill's preaching.

Hill went from raising hogs to raising souls from darkness. There was nothing impossible to him, because he believed on the One who sent him to this earth to do the will of God.

# GARRETT A. MORGAN—STILL SAVING LIVES TODAY

On July 24, 1916, thirty-two men were trapped in a tunnel beneath Lake Erie as a result of a huge explosion. There was no one who could rescue them from their calamity. Numerous unsuccessful attempts by local rescuers proved that their equipment was inadequate to save the men. There was no way to get around the smoke, dust, and poisonous gases.

Garrett Morgan was an inventor who was later heralded for his development of the traffic signal. He also had numerous other patents that turned into excellent sources of income for this young, African-American businessman. While resting is his home, the ring of his phone prompted the feat for which he is most remembered.

Immediately responding to the call, he rushed over to the site of the explosion with his brother, and into the tunnel. After a long delay, they emerged from the tunnel, carrying with them one rescued worker after another. The crowds around the tragic site were wild with applause. Lives were saved, and Garrett accomplished what no other man could do. He was able to brave the dangers of the gas and smoke-filled tunnel because he was the inventor of the piece of safety equipment that he and his brother wore as they rescued dozens of men. Garrett invented the gas mask, and this was the first time it had ever been used in any official capacity.

The life of this young businessman continued to flourish, as word of the gas mask spread across the city and country. Sadly, many of the orders for gas masks were canceled when buyers found out that Morgan was black. Still, this prejudice did not stop the United States military from utilizing Morgan's invention.

Today, the safety of millions of people worldwide depends upon the invention of the son of American slaves—Garrett Morgan. The gas mask and the traffic signal were the two greatest inventions of his life.

## RUFUS—A HERO IN BLACK SKIN

*Recently, a colored man who lives not many miles from the Tuskegee Normal and Industrial Institute, in Alabama, found that when he had harvested his cotton and paid all his debts he had about one hundred dollars remaining. This negro is now about sixty-five years of age, and of course spent a large portion of his early life in slavery. So far as book-learning is concerned, he is ignorant. Notwithstanding this, I have met few persons in all my acquaintance with whom I always feel that I can spend half an hour more profitably than with this seemingly uneducated member of my race. In his own community this man is known simply by the name of "Rufus."*

*On many occasions Rufus has talked with me about the need of education for young people. This subject seems to be continually in his thoughts.*

*After Rufus had harvested his crop, as I have said, and evidently had thought the matter over carefully, he appeared at my office one afternoon. As he entered I saw at a glance that he had something unusually weighty upon his mind, and I feared that there had been some misfortune in his family. He wore his usual rough garb of a farmer, and there were no frills in evidence about him. On that day he was simply himself—just plain Rufus, as he always is.*

*After considerable hesitation he came to the matter about which he wished to consult me. He asked if I would be willing to accept a small gift from him, to be used toward the education of one of our boys or girls. I told him that I should be delighted to accept the gift, if he felt that he could part with any of his hard-earned dollars. After searching in his rough garments for a little time, he finally produced from some hidden part of his clothes a rag around which a white cotton string was carefully tied. Unfastening the string slowly and with trembling fingers, he produced a ten-dollar bill, which he begged me to accept as his gift toward the education of some black boy or girl.*

*I have had the privilege of receiving many gifts for the Tuskegee Institute, but rarely one that has touched my heart and surprised me as this one did.*

*In a few minutes after having made his offering, Rufus left me and went to his home. The next day he sought out the principal of a white school in his own town, and after going through much the same performance as with me, placed a second ten-dollar bill in the hands of this white teacher, and begged him to use it toward the education of a white boy or girl.*[70]

---

# Sergeant William H. Carney—The Flag Never Touched the Ground

*During the Civil War in the course of the operations
before the city of Charleston, South Carolina, it was
decided to concentrate all the available forces of the
Federal army on Fort Wagner on Morris Island, in order
to bombard the fort, and then to charge it.*

*After an exhausting march, and without the troops
having had time for food, the bombardment began. The
line of battle was formed with the Fifty-fourth
Massachusetts assigned to the post of honor and danger,
in front of the attacking column.*

*Suddenly such a terrific fire was opened on the regiment
when ascending the wall of the fort with full ranks that,
using the words of Sergeant Carney, "they melted away
almost instantly" before the enemy's fire.*

*During the attack, Colonel Robert G. Shaw, commanding
the brigade, was killed. So disastrous was the fire that
the brigade was compelled to retire; but Sergeant Carney,
who was with the battalion in the lead of the storming
column, and who, with the regimental colors, had
pressed forward near the colonel leading the men over
the ditch, planted the flag upon the parapet, and, lying
down in order to get as much shelter as possible, for half
an hour, until the second brigade came up, kept the
colors up all the time. He received a severe wound in the*

*head. When this brigade retired, he, creeping on his knees, having by this time received a wound in the thigh also, followed them, but still holding up the flag. Thus he held the flag over the wall of Fort Wagner during the conflict of two brigades, and received two wounds.*

*When he entered the field hospital where his wounded comrades were, they cheered him and the colors. Nearly exhausted from the loss of blood, he exclaimed: "Boys, the old flag never touched the ground!"*[71]

## JOHN MATTHEWS—A PICTURE OF INTEGRITY

*Some years ago, when visiting a little town in western
Ohio, I found a colored man who made an impression
upon me which I shall never forget. This man's name was
Matthews. When I saw him he was about sixty years of
age. In early life he had been a slave in Virginia.*

*As a slave Matthews had learned the trade of a
carpenter, and his master, seeing that his slave could
earn more money for him by taking contracts in various
parts of the county in which he lived, permitted him to
go about to do so. Matthews, however, soon began to
reason, and naturally reached the conclusion that if he
could earn money for his master, he could earn it for
himself.*

*So, in 1858, or about that time, he proposed to his
master that he would pay fifteen hundred dollars for
himself, a certain amount to be paid in cash, and the
remainder in yearly installments. Such a bargain as this
was not uncommon in Virginia then. The master, having
implicit confidence in the slave, permitted him, after this
contract was made, to seek work wherever he could
secure the most pay. The result was that Matthews
secured a contract for the erection of a building in the
State of Ohio.*

*While the colored man was at work in Ohio the Union
armies were declared victorious, the Civil War ended,*

*and freedom came to him, as it did to four million other slaves.*

*When he was declared a free man by Abraham Lincoln's proclamation, Matthews still owed his former master, according to his ante-bellum contract, three hundred dollars. As Mr. Matthews told the story to me, he said that he was perfectly well aware that by Lincoln's proclamation he was released from all legal obligations, and that in the eyes of nine tenths of the world he was released from all moral obligations to pay his former master a single cent of the unpaid balance. But he said that he wanted to begin his life of freedom with a clean conscience. In order to do this, he walked from his home in Ohio, a distance of three hundred miles, much of the way over the mountains, and placed in his former master's hand every cent of the money that he had promised years before to pay him for his freedom.*[72]

# Rosa Parks—Mother of the Civil Rights Movement

There she stood, waiting for her bus to take her home from a hard day of work. She was tired—but her step onto the bus showed the world exactly what she was tired of. She noticed, as she usually did, the seats marked as "white only." State law prohibited her from sitting in those seats simply because she was African American. This day, she was not only African American. She was African American and exhausted. Rosa Parks sat in the middle of the bus.

As the ride continued, the bus grew more and more crowded with white passengers. Seeing this, the driver of the bus ordered the black passengers to the back of the bus to accommodate the new white passengers entering the bus. Rosa Parks was an active member of the NAACP at the time and was never one to break rules—even segregationist ones.

But on this day, perhaps she was tired from a hard day's work, or she was tired from a life of humiliation and segregation. Whatever the reason, Rosa did not budge.

The driver began to shout and threaten Rosa, even leaving his seat in order to intimidate her. Her simple response to his fuming threat was to simply refuse to move out of the seat. She was promptly arrested. Bail was posted for her release, but the story was far from over.

Local black leaders decided to boycott the bus system and

called upon a popular twenty-six-year-old minister to lead the boycott. He was an unassuming young man, who did not have much influence at the time. But soon, his name would become synonymous with the Civil Rights Movement. Martin Luther King Jr. rose to the occasion.

Rosa Parks was fined fourteen dollars for her "crime." And because she believed it to be an unjust law, she refused to pay it. Compromise can come in small packages, but the destruction of such compromise can be huge.

The boycott continued in earnest nearly two weeks later. Martin Luther King Jr. oversaw the boycott, and on December fifth, the protestors waited near a bus stop to see if their boycott was a success. It was. No African Americans rode the buses. They took carpools, rode bicycles, and walked to work instead of riding the city buses. The plan worked, and the Civil Rights Movement began.

Under the leadership of Martin Luther King Jr., civil rights advocates began a nationwide push towards racial equality. But if it hadn't been for a humble seamstress named Rosa Parks, many of the rights that African Americans enjoy today could very well be nonexistent.

# ENDNOTES

1. Mahalia Jackson and Evan McLeod Wylie, *Movin Up,* Hawthorn Books, 1966.

2. http://www.amherst.edu/~aardoc/Betsey_Stockton_Journal_1.html (paragraph 7, line 4).

3. Ibid.

4. *Religious Experience and Journal of Mrs. Jarena Lee, Giving an Account of Her Call to Preach the Gospel, revised and corrected from the original manuscript, written by herself,* Philadelphia: 1849.

5. *Memoir of Old Elizabeth, A Coloured Woman.*

6. Henry Box Brown, *Narrative of the Life of Henry Box Brown, Written by himself,* Manchester: Printed by Lee and Glynn, 1851.

7. Ibid.

8. Ibid.

9. John Marrant, *Narrative of John Marrant,*1785.

10. http://collections.ic.gc.ca/blackloyalists/documents/diaries/marrant_narrative. htm

11. *An Account of Life of Mr. David George from S.L.A. given by himself.*

12. Ibid.

13. Boston King, *The Memoirs of Boston King,* 1794.

14. Ibid.

15. http://www.infoplease.com/ce6/people/A0820235.html

16. Taken from Henry Garnett's second speech to the United States House of Representatives, 1843.

17. http://www.pbs.org/wgbh/aia/part4/4h2937t.html

18. http://www.wheaton.edu/bgc/archives/docs/waite.htm

19. http://www.loc.gov/bicentennial/propage/AL/al-1_h_callahan1.html

20. Ibid.

21. Fred Brown, Liberty Prison Ministries.

22. *A Treasury of Catholic Reading,* ed. John Chapin, Farrar, Straus and Cudahy, 1957.

23. *Mrs. Stewart's Farewell Address to Her Friends in the City of Boston,* delivered September 21, 1833.

24. Ibid.

25. *Incidents in the Life of the Reverend. J. Asher, Pastor of Shiloh (Coloured)*

Baptist Church, Philadelphia, and a Concluding Chapter of Facts Illustrating the Unrighteous Prejudice Existing in the Minds of American Citizens toward Their Coloured Brethren.

26. Ibid.

27. Fugitive Slave Act of 1850, Sections 1-10.

28. The Rev. J. W. Loguen, *As a Slave and As a Freeman: A Narrative of Real Life*, Syracuse, NY: J. G. K. Truair & Co., Stereotypers and Printers Office of the Daily Journal, 1859.

29. *Recollections of Seventy Years, by Bishop Daniel Alexander Payne, D. D., LL. D., Senior Bishop of the African Methodist Episcopal Church*, Nashville, TN: Publishing House of the AME Sunday School Union, 1888.

30. Ibid.

31. *Autobiography of Bishop Isaac Lane, LL.D.with a Short History of the C.M.E. Church in America and of Methodism.*

32. Ibid.

33. *The Story of the Lord's Dealings with Mrs. Amanda Smith the Colored Evangelist, Containing an Account of Her Life Work of Faith, and Her Travels in America, England, Ireland, Scotland, India, and Africa as an Independent Missionary*, 1893.

34. Ibid.

35. Ibid.

36. *Light in the Dark Belt*, Concordia Publishing House, 1951.

37. Ibid.

38. *From Ocean to Ocean, 1918-1919: A Record of the Work of the Women's American Baptist Home Mission Society.*

39. *Journal of the Twentieth Annual Session of the Woman's Convention Auxiliary to the National Baptist Convention*, 1920.

40. Frederick Douglass, *My Bondage and My Freedom. Part I—Life As a Slave. Part II—Life As a Freeman*, 1855. p. 166.

41.Raleigh H. Merritt, *From Capivity to Fame or The Life of George Washington Carver*, Boston, Mass: Meador Pub. Co., 1929.

42. *Memoir and Poems of Phillis Wheatley, a Native African and a Slave, Dedicated to the Friends of the Africans.*

43. Phyllis Wheatley, *Poems on Various Subjects Religious and Moral*, 1773.

44. *Memoir and Poems of Phillis Wheatley, a Native African and a Slave, Dedicated to the Friends of the Africans.*

45. Ibid.

46. Les Brown

47. Sojourner Truth, Olive Gilbert, and Frances Titus, *Narrative of Sojourner Truth—a Bondswoman of Olden Time, Emancipated by the New York Legislature in the Early Part of the Present Century; with a History of Her Labors and Correspondence Drawn from Her "Book of Life;" Also, a Memorial Chapter, Giving the Particulars of Her Last Sickness and Death.* p. 67.

48. Richard Allen, *The Life, Experience, and Gospel Labours of the Rt. Rev. Richard Allen to Which is Annexed the Rise and Progress of the African Methodist Episcopal Church in the United States of America. Containing a Narrative of the Yellow Fever in the Year of Our Lord 1793 with an Address to the People of Colour in the United States,* p. 28.

49. Ibid.

50. Ibid.

51. Ibid.

52. Booker T. Washington, *Dedication Speech at Tuskagee Institute,* July 4, 1881.

53. E. A. Randolph, *The Life of Rev. John Jasper, Pastor of Sixth Mt. Zion Baptist Church, Richmond, Va. from His Birth to the Present Time, with His Theory on the Rotation of the Sun,* Richmond, VA: R. T. Hill & Co., Publishers, 1884, p. 129.

54. http://docsouth.unc.edu/neh/meachum/meachum.html

55. John Meachum, *An Address to All the Colored Citizens of the United States,* pp. 9-10.

56. Thomas L. Johnson, *Twenty-Eight Years a Slave or The Story of My Life in Three Continents,* Bournemouth, Eng.: W. Mate & Sons, 1909.

57. Ibid.

58. Ibid.

59. Martin Luther King Jr., *Speech at the March on Washington,* 1963.

60. Martin Luther King Jr., *Letter from a Birmingham Jail.*

61. Colin Powell with Joseph E. Persico, *My American Journey,* Ballentine Books; Reprint Edition, July 1, 1996.

62. Wilson Armistead, *A Tribute for the Negro:Being a Vindication of the Moral, Intellectual, and Religious Capabilities of the Coloured Portion of Mankind; with Particular Reference to the African Race,* 1848.

63. Ibid.

64. J.H.B. Latrobe, *Biography of Elder Lott Cary,Late Missionary to Africa, With an Appendix on the Subject of Colonization*, James B. Taylor.

65. Ibid.

66. Wilson Armistead, *A Tribute for the Negro:Being a Vindication of the Moral, Intellectual, and Religious Capabilities of the Coloured Portion of Mankind; with Particular Reference to the African Race*, 1848.

67. Ibid.

68. E.V. Hill, *A Savior Worth Having*, Moody Press, 2002.

69. Ibid.

70. Booker T. Washington, "Heroes in Black Skins," *Century Magazine*, New York, September 1903.

71. Ibid.

72. Ibid.

Additional copies of this book and other titles by Honor Books are available from your local bookstore.

Also available in the African American Heritage Series:

*Soul Cry: Powerful Prayers from the Spiritual Heritage of African Americans*

*Soul Praise: Amazing Stories Behind the Great African American Hymns and Negro Spirituals*

*Voices of Hope: Timeless Expressions of Faith from African Americans*

If you have enjoyed this book, or if it has impacted your life, we would like to hear from you.

Please contact us at:

Honor Books,

An imprint of Cook Communications Ministries

4050 Lee Vance View

Colorado Springs, CO 80918

www.cookministries.com